Contents

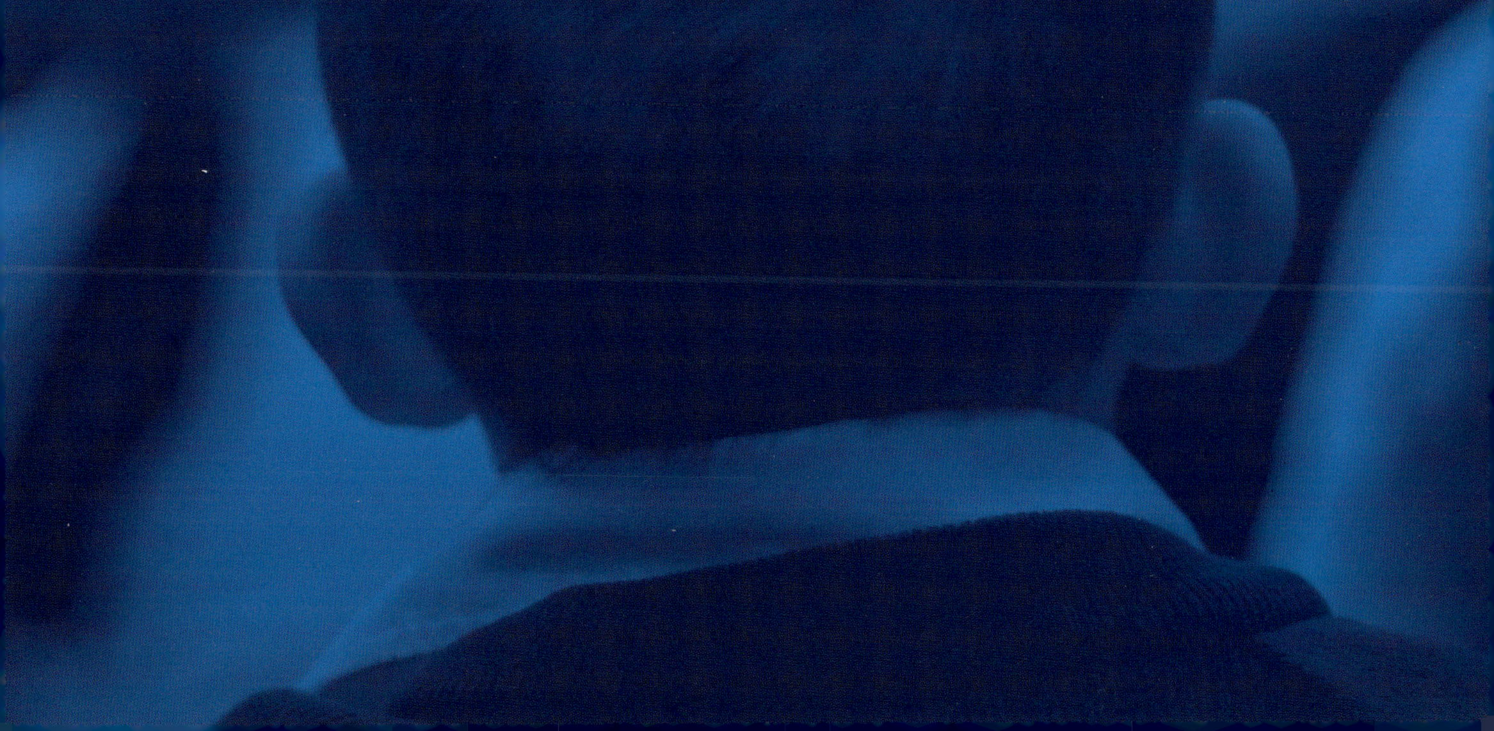

1. Introduction
Concept image and Numicon

In order to make the best use of Numicon it is helpful to understand the purposes of the Numicon images. They were designed to exploit three strengths to help pupils understand number: learning from action, learning from seeing, and sense of pattern. The Numicon images are designed to allow pupils to manipulate, observe and notice, and explore pattern. They are designed to help pupils see connections between numbers through manipulating and making connections between images. The key idea for pupils to understand is that numbers do not occur randomly, but that they are part of a highly organised system – filled with many kinds of patterns.

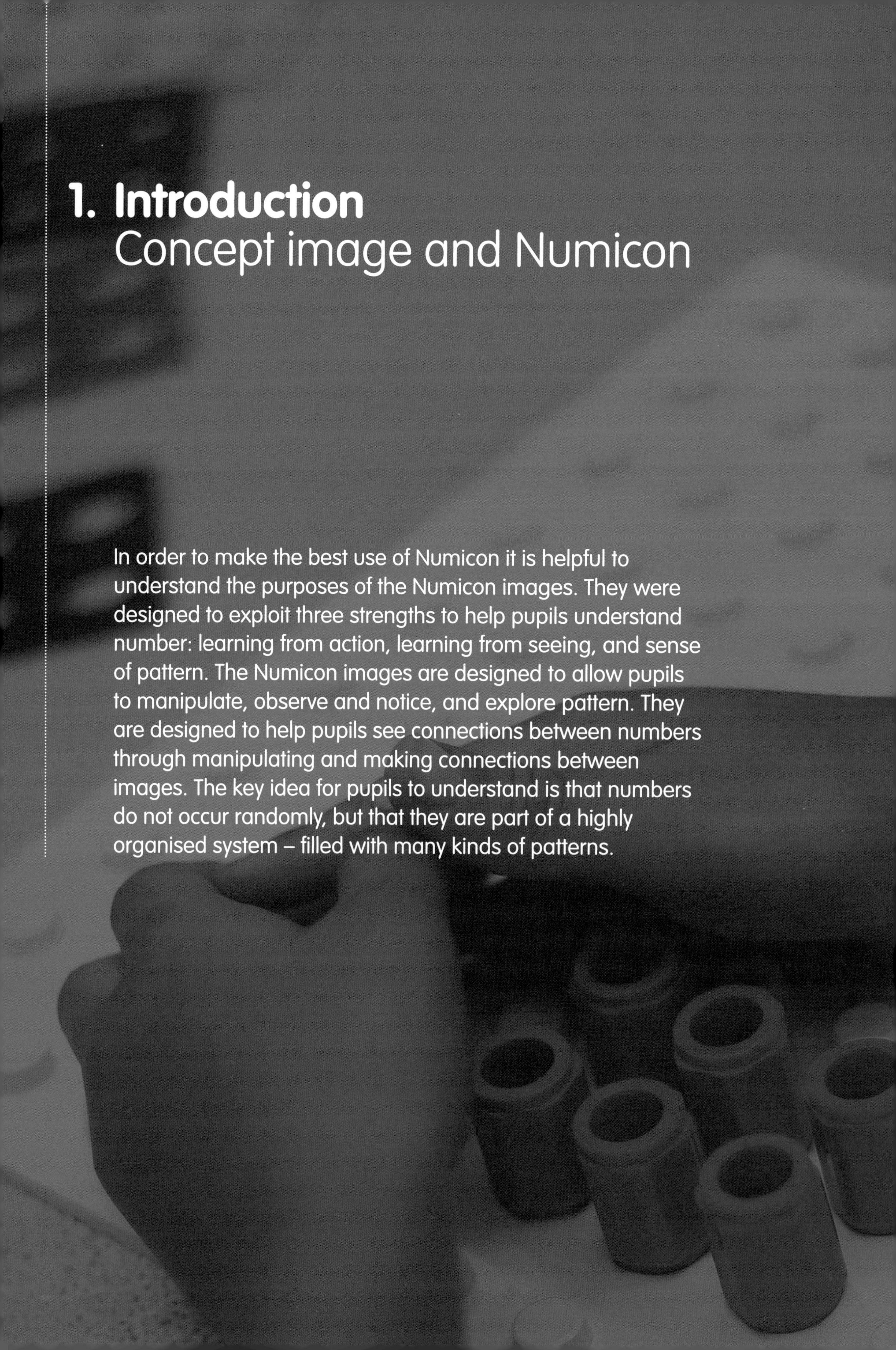

The *Closing the Gap with Numicon* kit has been designed specifically for pupils experiencing significantly greater difficulty learning mathematics than the majority of pupils of their age. This kit is an important step in our ongoing work with Numicon (which originated in a teacher research project with mixed ability Foundation and Key Stage 1 classes) (Atkinson et al., 2004) and has been produced in response to requests for ideas for using Numicon to teach pupils who are experiencing difficulty and pupils who have special educational needs (SEN). Pupils experience difficulties for many reasons. They may have underlying cognitive difficulties that make the acquisition and retention of mathematical understanding problematic; they may have linguistic or sensory problems that hinder their access to learning. There may be personal, social and emotional factors that are having an impact on a pupil's approach to learning. Pupils may have missed periods of schooling; suffered periods of ineffective teaching; have specific gaps in their mathematical understanding; or have a first language that is not English.

Some pupils' difficulties may warrant their being described as having SEN, which affect their ability to learn mathematics. These difficulties can be related to:

- difficulties with numerosity (sometimes described as dyscalculia);
- Speech, Language and Communication Needs (SLCN), specific learning difficulties (including dyslexia);
- general/global cognitive difficulties (i.e., moderate, severe or profound and multiple learning difficulties);
- pervasive developmental disorders (e.g., Autistic Spectrum Condition (ASC) including Aspergers Syndrome);
- sensory impairments;
- specific conditions (e.g., Down Syndrome, etc.).

Although it offers guidance on some of the issues that relate to specific SEN categories, the main objective of this kit is to address pupils' difficulties in learning and accessing mathematics irrespective of how their difficulties are described. We strongly recommend that teachers avoid labelling a pupil's needs in order to match them with strategies assigned to that label. Instead we would urge that (in collaboration with colleagues), the teacher should construct a profile of the pupil's strengths and difficulties and then evaluate how Numicon can be used to address them[1].

The aim of this kit is to enable pupils to develop a foundation of basic number understanding, and to give all pupils a positive experience of learning mathematics. A sound basis of number understanding is essential for pupils to achieve their individual potential and to understand money, time and measures and to handle everyday data if this is within their capability. Some pupils will move quickly through the activities and gain insights that resolve previous misconceptions. Other pupils' progress will be slower because of their significantly greater difficulties with the concepts. Research has shown[2] that the majority of pupils rapidly gain in confidence when they start working with Numicon, and those with the potential to acquire mathematical understanding readily move on to Numicon Kits 1 and 2 after working through the activities in this kit, resulting in the ability to engage in maths lessons successfully alongside their age peers.

Numicon is designed for inclusive practice.[3] The use of clear visual models and images benefits all pupils learning mathematics, including high achievers. The basic number ideas addressed in this kit would not normally be taught as part of a daily mathematics lesson for older pupils, although all the activities can be practised as small group work within the lesson. It may be appropriate under some circumstances, for pupils to work out of the classroom, either individually or in small groups.

1 The pro-forma included with the Assessment Tools is intended to assist in the construction of a profile of mathematical strengths and difficulties.
2 Refer to the Numicon website www.numicon.com for details of independent research projects.
3 See Department for Education and Skills (DfES) National Curriculum Inclusion Statement www.nc.uk.net/nc_resources/html/inclusion.shtml, accessed 1.8.2008.

This Teaching Guide is intended as a reference for all those involved in teaching pupils who are experiencing difficulties with mathematics. It aims to give teachers an understanding of the underlying problems and difficulties pupils may experience in accessing mathematical learning, as a result perhaps of memory difficulties, wider cognitive difficulties (global learning difficulties); language difficulties, spatial difficulties, motor-co-ordination difficulties and visual or hearing impairments. It aims to foster appreciation in all pupils of the crucial importance of a positive and engaging experience with mathematics learning.

The Teaching Programme should be used in combination with the Teaching Guide to provide practical solutions to pupils' difficulties and to support teachers in their assessment, planning and teaching. The focus of the Numicon teaching approach is progressive development of a deep understanding among pupils of the essential building blocks of mathematical attainment; to this end, the Teaching Activities have been organised in small steps to address specific potential areas of difficulty. There are suggestions for smaller steps and extensions to help teachers set suitable learning challenges related to individual pupils' stages of mathematical development. The Teaching Programme is designed to be followed sequentially, alongside ongoing work from the sections on Counting and Pattern. It follows the typical acquisition of early number skills, addressing the achievement of numerosity (awareness of the number of objects in a set), counting, the ability to recognise and exploit pattern, and early computation.

Pupils with no experience of Numicon will need to start with the first activities in this kit and progress through the Teaching Programme at a speed dictated by them. Some pupils may progress very quickly and achieve the potential to work at the level of their age peers. Once they have achieved competence with the basic ideas addressed in this kit, the suggestions for extension are likely to be appropriate for these pupils. Pupils who take longer to assimilate the ideas will likely benefit from following the smaller steps suggested for each activity.

There are three Assessment for Learning Tools. First, a simple checklist called 'Numicon Assessment Signposts', which helps to identify gaps in pupils' understanding within the Programme of Activities and to plan the next steps. Second, the Profiling Pro Forma, which is designed to help teachers identify pupils' strengths and areas of difficulty. And third, the Individual Record of Progress, which is linked to the very small steps within the Teaching Programme and is useful for tracking pupils' progress. It is essential that pupils experiencing difficulties with mathematics develop a firm grasp of the principles of pattern, order, counting and place value if they are to achieve later success in mathematics. Therefore, all pupils must be competent in the core activities covered in this kit before moving on to the work in Kits 1 and 2.

Concept image

It is important to remember that Numicon images are not designed to be used in isolation: children should have a range of number experiences, within which Numicon images will be significant. The aim is to develop rich 'concept images'. For example, it is difficult to define a formal concept for 'five'. We can count to five; we can give a child five sweets; we can point to a pattern of five spots on a domino; we can tell the child she is five; we can listen to 'Five Live' radio; we can sing about five speckled frogs; we can read the Famous Five books; we can talk about (and show) 'one less than six', 'one more than four', ' half of ten', and '2 + 3', etc. We can offer children experiences with 'five', that link together, if only through repetition of the word 'five'. This totality of impressions is referred to as the 'concept image for five'. Children experiencing difficulties learning mathematics may require small step, progressive experiences in order to acquire rich concept images, which incorporate Numicon images within a broad and systematic experience of number.

Children form impressions and ideas, acquire techniques and skills, form associations and accumulate experiences, which add up to their continually developing individual mental impressions of mathematical ideas. It is these mental impressions that dominate their thinking and it is these individual, developing mental impressions or concept images that, as teachers, we seek to influence (see figure 1).

To return to the several examples for the number five, for many pupils with difficulties learning mathematics, the fact that the word 'five' can invite so many associations is initially confusing and is a barrier to their acquisition of the cardinal meaning (size) of 5. Effective concept images for numbers, which can be semantically linked, are of critical importance for learning mathematics. Numicon's emphasis on developing systematic visual patterns is central for supporting the attempts of children with difficulties learning mathematics to organise their developing mental impressions into a systematic understanding of the number system.

We do not want to restrict children's concept images to Numicon visual patterns, but this powerful visual patterning enables the development of rich and broad concept images, particularly when Numicon is used alongside augmentative and alternative communication strategies, such as Makaton®, in which concepts, including number, are also represented with manual signs and pictorial symbols. The concept image for any particular number should consist of interrelated representations:

- the Numicon patterned visual image (shape);
- its position on the number line;
- its numeral;
- its name (both the spoken and the written word);
- images, using random arrangements for the number counting experiences;
- 'everyday life' interpretations;
- a manual sign.

Particularly useful additions to the above experiences are images and actions associated with Number Rods.[4] In our work with children we have used Number Rods alongside the imagery listed above and found that pupils can incorporate these very effectively to give yet another structured dimension to their understanding of number (see figure 2).

For children experiencing difficulties, it may be necessary to teach these aspects of the concept image progressively, through structured and graded learning experiences, rather than through total immersion in all aspects from the beginning.

Fig 1: The Numicon number line helps pupils to relate the Numicon Shape with its position on the number line, the numeral and the number word. Pupils can also see the relationship between the images.

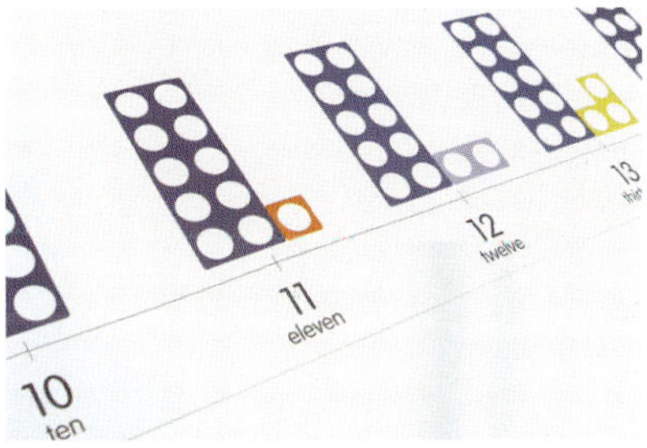

Fig 2: Number Rods offer pupils another structured representation of number ideas.

[4] A Numicon product available from Numicon Ltd.

2. **Key mathematical ideas** Difficulties that pupils may have in acquiring understanding

The National Curriculum for England and Wales acknowledges learning mathematics involves more than learning certain facts and calculation techniques; it includes learning how to use mathematics in practical situations and learning about mathematics as an *activity* (see also Section 4). Therefore, as pupils learn about number and calculation, they need also to learn how to do mathematics. There are several elements involved in thinking mathematically, most stemming directly from the essentially abstract character of mathematical ideas. Probably the most fundamental aspect of mathematical thinking is the need to be *logical* when dealing with abstract ideas; without logic we cannot trust the outcome of our thinking, that is, our conclusions.

In this section

Mathematical thinking

Piaget (1952) teaches us that young pupils do not think logically – in the way that most adults are able to do, and that their gradual progress toward adult logical thinking is partly experiential, partly maturational. We cannot expect young pupils to think like adults, but we can discuss their thinking with them and help them to reflect on the reasoning behind it.

Pupils' earliest mathematical reasoning should be shared, explored and reflected upon; young pupils (and some children with special needs) will not frame clear, logical arguments, but it is important that they understand that the way they think matters to us, and that 'thinking' is worth thinking about. For pupils to be willing, and increasingly able, to share and develop their mathematical thinking, they need to feel confident that their thoughts are welcomed, respected and important; if their ideas are dismissed as 'wrong' or low-level, or are ridiculed, this will make pupils close up and lose faith in their abilities. Central to the Numicon approach is building confidence in mathematical thinking and reasoning; it is important to exploit every opportunity to nurture these abilities in pupils and provide them with a supportive environment.

Fig 1: Using the Baseboard as a frame to organise different combinations of Shapes to make 6.

The relationship between language and thinking has been much debated by philosophers, linguists and psychologists among others, but there is a consensus that thought and language are closely linked. People who experience difficulties learning mathematics often have problems with speech, language and communication even when they have not been categorised as having 'speech and language difficulties' or 'specific language impairment'. And speech, language and communication difficulties underlie many SEN. Because of the close relationship between language and thought, pupils with language needs will require additional support in developing mathematical thinking, in the form of:

1. modelling of mathematical thinking by the teacher;
2. scaffolding of the pupil or young person's thinking in relation to a particular mathematical task, through the provision of a visual framework of the sequence of thinking activities needed to solve a particular mathematical task;
3. supportive correction of erroneous or unhelpful thinking, ensuring that the pupil is not left feeling that his or her approach was completely 'wrong'.

Another fundamental characteristic of mathematical thinking is the focus on generalising. It is important to look for patterns in all situations; when a pattern is identified it is possible to generalise and predict. Teachers should encourage generalisation by taking every opportunity to enquire: 'Do you think that this will *always* happen?'

It is also essential for pupils to approach situations systematically. Being systematic is an aspect of effective reasoning and provides a foundation for generalising (and thus predicting). Working with Numicon provides many opportunities to encourage pupils to work systematically; there are frames included in the set of master sheets to help pupils organise their work in certain activities (see figure 1). Teaching Activity 13b specifically invites pupils to think systematically about possibilities, to resist the impulse to make wild guesses, and to have the patience to explore in detail what *could* happen, before reaching any conclusions.

The final element of mathematical thinking is the ability to use and apply abstract mathematical ideas in real situations. The Teaching Activities signal opportunities for teachers to help pupils to connect their developing understanding of mathematical ideas with their everyday world.

Using and applying mathematics requires the ability to understand and use mathematical skills, concepts and knowledge *framed in spoken or written language*. If pupils have language needs, they will need extra support to learn how to apply and use mathematics. Section 5, Using and Applying Mathematics – including everyday functioning, provides some useful strategies.

It should be remembered that mathematical thinking continues to be important throughout pupils' mathematics learning, and is an integral part of their mathematical experience. How pupils think about their mathematical activities should be a reflection of the key elements identified above.

Fig 2: Pupils are encouraged to copy, continue and devise repeating patterns with a variety of apparatus.

Fig 3: The Number Rod Trays give pupils a frame within which they can construct staircase patterns with Number Rods.

Pattern

Pupils are generally very able at perceiving patterns; without the ability to spot regularities in the world they cannot make sense of or learn from their experiences. Patterns make the world predictable, and pattern underlies mathematics. Pupils who have difficulties perceiving patterns are likely to have great difficulty in learning mathematics. Those who have specific linguistic difficulties can often spot visual patterns, but pupils with more general learning difficulties may also find this difficult, and need activities that are scaffolded in such a way that pattern is more easily perceivable. Numicon images offer several kinds of visual patterns suggesting connections between numbers: because these patterns are visual they provide pupils who have mathematical learning difficulties greater opportunities for success. The better the pupil's ability to identify patterns and connect numbers to them, the better he or she will be able to exploit these connections to calculate efficiently (see figure 2).

Order

The most important regularity in number is order. Pupils need to be able to make the vital connection between 'one more-ness' and 'next-ness' to understand the system of whole numbers. To make this connection and use it in mathematical thinking, it is helpful to learn the linguistic labels 'one more' and 'next' *within the context of number*. The patterned images in this pack (i.e., the Numicon Shapes) are designed to offer a systematic way of seeing how each 'next' number is 'one more' than the last, and of learning and retaining the meaning of the words 'next' and 'one more', in a mathematical context. Pupils are enabled to interpret what teachers and peers say (their words), by noting the relative sizes of the Numicon Shapes. The structure of the Shapes should enable pupils to begin to sense alternating 'oddness' and 'evenness'. Associating ordered structured patterns with the early number line introduces a visual image that will persist. Constructing 'staircase' patterns with Number Rods provides an image for 'one more' and, since for many pupils climbing stairs is accompanied by counting, making the connections among stairs, counting, Number Rods and number is usually straightforward (see figure 3).

Counting

Counting is usually a pupil's first experience of numbers in use. Counting is complex and its learning requires time and lots of practice. Pupils with speech and language needs and/or motor difficulties are likely to find counting particularly challenging because of the difficulties they experience in learning and retaining verbal sequences, producing speech, and/or co-coordinating the fine and gross motor sequencing required for manual counting (i.e., articulating the number names at the same speed and rhythm as their manual count of objects). Two of the Activity Cards in this kit address counting; these activities should be ongoing alongside all the other Activity Cards.

It is recommended that counting activities for pupils with difficulties should be scaffolded in such a way as to ensure there is no repetition of inaccurate counting, and to help their understanding that the ultimate number name used describes the total number of objects. To help with this, this kit includes Photocopy Masters of counting frames, number tracks and number lines. It is important to remember that there is a difference between 'just' counting (reciting number names in order) and 'counting things' to discover how many there are. *Both* activities are vital for pupils' mathematical experience, but the latter is much more difficult to comprehend. By reciting number names pupils can begin to sense patterns within the number naming system; by counting objects pupils are learning the most basic use of numbers to identify 'how many', that is, the value of any count (see figure 4). For pupils with *motor co-ordination difficulties* it is *essential* to consider the *size* and the *spacing* of the objects used in counting activities. It is important not to underestimate how much pupils learn about mathematical significance from the experience of counting (e.g., that numbers are ordered, that each next number represents 'one more' than the last, that numbers can go on for ever, that there is a system to the way we count, etc.). Counting activities should be accompanied by use of Numicon Shapes and visual references to printed number lines. In the Assessment section of this Teachers Book there is guidance on how to assess counting; it is important that these assessments continue until pupils are secure in their knowledge and understanding of the count sequence and can count forward and back from any number. It cannot be assumed that because a pupil is able to count accurately from one to a hundred, and appears to understand grouping in thousands, hundreds, tens and units, there is no necessity for him or her to be able to count on in ones, say from 2,987 to 3,005. Many pupils need to practise these types of counts frequently.

Fig 4: Counting by placing objects one by one on the Numicon Number Line.

To count or not

It is also important for pupils to be able to know when to count and when *not to count;* this will differ according to levels of mathematical skills and knowledge, and circumstances. A key feature of Numicon is that children calculate *without* counting, by using the Shapes as whole numbers. In the early stages of working with Numicon pupils learn to show addition by combining Numicon Shapes and to show subtraction either by comparing two Shapes to show difference, or by hiding part of a Shape to show 'take away'. Using Numicon Shapes in this way helps children to memorise addition and subtraction facts. Once a pupil can use Numicon Shapes and has memorised the addition facts of ten, it is inefficient for them to count on their fingers. However, pupils who have learnt previously to perform simple addition and subtraction by counting objects (or fingers) are likely to revert to this in problem solving situations – so it may be necessary to remind them that they have already mastered the mathematics needed to solve the particular problem, and to help them recall and apply the number facts that they know to the problem at hand.

Pupils with mathematics learning difficulties are often unaware of what they know, and do not understand how what they do know can be applied in various mathematical situations. Also, pupils with learning difficulties frequently feel obliged to count, and it may be necessary to stop them from counting and to show them how they can apply what they know. Pupils must learn to recognise when counting is inefficient or unnecessary, for example, when a set of objects is sufficiently small that they can subitise (i.e., perceive at a glance the number of objects in a set) and when it is appropriate to group objects into Numicon patterns to find out 'how many without counting' as described in Activity 8b. They must be made aware that it is *the correct answer not the counting behaviour,* that is the objective. It may also be necessary to demonstrate, using appropriate language, that an answer can be determined via a variety of methods: counting, subitising, grouping or, in the case of an addition or subtraction problem, recalling the number fact.

Seeing numbers as wholes

It is through counting activities that pupils begin to develop their early understanding of number, but it is important to understand that their progress into arithmetic depends upon their ability to go beyond counting to seeing numbers as 'wholes'. It is not helpful for 'six' to be viewed as part of the chain 'one-two-three-four-five-six' when calculating because in order to calculate efficiently 'six' needs to be understood as a whole number idea. Many pupils with learning and/or language difficulties find it easier to understand the 'wholeness' of a number, and how it relates to other numbers (e.g. how the 'whole' 10 is made up of various 'sub-wholes', e.g. the 'sub-wholes' 4 and 6), than a number's position within a sequence. Numicon images have been designed to help pupils see numbers as clear 'wholes', to see 'six' (for example) as an organised pattern that is whole and complete in itself (but a pattern, that with the pattern for four, can also make up part of the 'whole' of ten). Pupils need to compress their understanding of the six 'ones' that make up six in counting, into a whole, composite idea called 'six'.

Fig 5: Arranging Numicon Pegs into the Numicon pattern to see the value of the count.

The system of patterns in the Numicon images is designed to show pupils how each individual 'whole' number relates to other 'whole' numbers. This series of patterns (unlike domino or dice patterns) makes a whole four look like 'one less than five', 'one more than three', and 'two twos' whilst also allowing the distinctive patterns for 2, 3, 4 and 5 also to be memorable. It is seeing these patterns of relationships between whole numbers that constitutes the foundations of arithmetic, patterns that allow, for example, $4 + 4 = 8$ to make sense without counting. Numicon images are designed to help pupils 'see' how many things there are by arranging them into systematic, recognisable patterns, allowing them to 'see' numbers of things as organised wholes. For pupils to progress beyond counting they need to learn how to find out how many objects are in collections *without counting,* not just by subitising small sets of objects, but by arranging objects into patterns. *Patterns* are the key: constructing recognisable patterns enables pupils to 'see' how many objects there are without counting them; to compress lots of little bits into organised wholes (see figure 5).

Number Rods are designed to encourage pupils to see numbers as wholes, which is why they are not divided into '1s' with marks on the rods. Number Rods almost compel pupils to see numbers as wholes in relation to each other, since it is impossible to give any single rod a value by itself – numerical values can only be ascribed by comparing rods with each other. We need to avoid for example, teaching pupils that the red rod *only ever* means '2'. So whilst it would be possible to teach children that each rod represents only one number value (based upon how many '1s' fit along it), to do so would defeat the overall teaching purpose of concentrating upon *relationships between rods* and constrain the potential of the rods in later work when pupils learn that any numbers can be ascribed to individual rods. It is the relations between rods that is fundamental to understanding arithmetic.

Numbers, grouping in 10s and place value notation

Pupils need to understand the systematic naming of numbers. As has been demonstrated, it is essential that pupils master counting. This involves learning to handle an infinite set of names for numbers, and in the right order. Unfortunately for pupils trying to learn number names, in our society we use two parallel systems for naming numbers which sometimes conflict. We use *numerals* (a highly efficient specific written symbolic system for numbers, derived from Arabic) and *words,* a spoken and written verbal system (derived from the Germanic languages) to read, write and say numbers. Individually, these two systems are difficult for pupils to understand; the fact that they seem to conflict with one another makes learning a really complex task. It is unfortunate that the way we write names for numbers in numerals up to 30, and the way we say those number names up to 'thirty' are very different, and it is these number names that pupils meet most often early in their learning. The most frequent conflicts arise in relation to the names of the smaller 'teen' numbers, which pupils encounter after they have mastered the number names one to ten, and where there is no discernable pattern to the sounds of the words at all. An additional difficulty is that many of the English words for numbers are phonologically very similar – e.g., thirt*een* and thirty.)

Let us first consider the symbolic written code for numerals that pupils need to learn. Interestingly, civilization has been quite clever in devising a system for generating symbolic number names that not only allows us to construct new names, *ad infinitum,* but tells us instantly whereabouts in the series of number names any particular name belongs. For example, when we read '273' we know that it is the name of the number that follows 272, and is one hundred before 373. It is not necessary for us to remember every individual symbolic number name and its place in the order (which would be impossible since their number is infinite); we need only to understand the system that generates the names. The number system we use today took thousands of years to evolve; it is not surprising, therefore, that it can take some time for pupils to master it, especially those who have learning and/or language difficulties. Acquiring the skill of counting involves seeing a pattern, or rather several interlocking patterns, which may make it appear deceptively simple. Seeing patterns, therefore, is a powerful ability; patterns are key to doing most mathematics.

Grouping in 10s

There are two essential ideas underlying the symbolic system for naming numbers. The first is grouping. The number we call 'ten' (in numerals, 10) is the most important number in our naming system. When we count collections, once we have (in a group) ten of something, we call it one of something else. So ten 'ones' are called one 'ten'; ten 'tens' are called one 'hundred'. In the language we use, we group things into tens (and group groups) and call them one of something else. A key feature of Numicon is the way that the design of the Numicon number Shapes allows combinations of shapes, to be grouped together to make the 10 shape.

When we ask pupils to 'find how many' objects there are in a collection it is important always to help them physically group collections of objects into tens (and to group any remaining objects in the corresponding Numicon number pattern) as they try to find out how many things they have before them.[1] It is important to remember that many pupils with difficulties learning mathematics have organisational difficulties and for these pupils, the physical grouping of collections into tens may pose problems for their ideational (establishing an internal visual/motor representation) and motor execution (executing a motor plan to realise a representation) ability levels. Pupils with organisational difficulties may benefit from having the grouping process modelled for them, and having extra practice at undertaking grouping activities independently. Using the Numicon Shapes will help them to perceive groups, and to be able to perceive each group of ten as a distinct entity, different from the other groups of ten (in order to work out the cardinality of sets).

For some pupils, to be able to perceive each group of ten as a distinct entity, they may need to be taught specifically to organise sets of objects systematically (e.g., through initially placing their objects into left-to-right or top-to-bottom lines) and then to arrange them into Numicon patterns. Simply counting, one at a time, can easily become merely just a blind memory task for pupils struggling to remember which number name comes next. However, 'finding how many' by *grouping in tens* (and then

[1] Activity 8b

perhaps tens of tens), using the Numicon Shapes, is a constant reminder that our way of naming numbers uses a ten-based system, which is not only crucial for successful counting, but also for understanding many calculation techniques (see figure 6).

Place value

The second essential idea is *place value*; in a string of digits, the position or 'place' of each digit signifies its 'value'. Thus, the position of the '2' in the string '427' tells us it has the value of two tens. It is important to realise that 'place value' refers to an arbitrary *symbolic language* for naming and reading number names, which pupils need to understand. It can be difficult to learn because it is alien to non-mathematical contexts. To paraphrase Eva Grauberg,[2] when a child goes to bed with a cuddly toy, and the toy is held in her right arm and the child lies on her right side, if she turns onto her left side with the toy still in her arm, the toy does not become ten toys merely because it is now in a different place.

Fig 6: Finding how many by grouping in tens.

In the Numicon approach to 'finding how many', pupils are encouraged to develop their counting skills, and to understand that how we deal with (i.e., name) ever larger numbers is crucially dependent upon a grouping-in-tens system, which uses a 'place value' code. It is vital that pupils understand, for example, that the number name 'thirty' does not only represent the number that is one bigger than 29, but also is three groups of ten (represented clearly in Numicon by three ten patterns). In the Numicon activity 'Finding how many without counting' pupils are helped to develop techniques not just of counting in ones, but also of grouping in tens, which introduces them to the 'place value' code.

Number lines have an important role in helping pupils to understand place value, although, those experiencing difficulty with mathematics often find the sequential organisation of number lines particularly difficult. However, the Numicon 0–21 number line helps pupils to understand its sequential aspect through the changing *cardinality* of the numbers, which is represented by Numicon images and displayed above the numerals in the number line. This Numicon number line also helps pupils to notice how numbers greater than ten can be partitioned; for example, 16 is presented as a 10 and a 6, giving pupils a visual support which can be more helpful than the verbal '1 ten and 6 units' interpretation, which is common in some approaches to written arithmetic. Further reinforcement of the tens structure of our number naming system is afforded by number lines, which use alternating colours to show decade divisions (see figure 7).

Fig 7: Building a number line from 21 with Numicon Shapes.

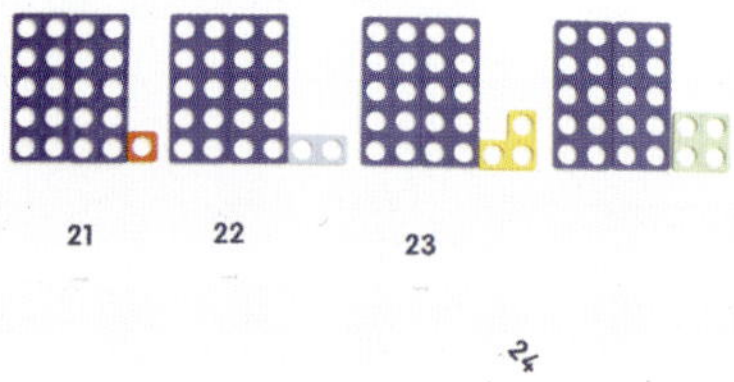

It cannot be assumed that if a pupil has understanding of the symbolic system for labelling numbers with numerals he or she also understands the parallel verbal system for naming numbers, because the latter is based on arbitrary linguistic *conventions*, not logic. The words 'ten', 'eleven', and 'twelve' do not signal that anything significant happens when we count beyond nine, whereas the symbolic numeral code '10', '11', and '12' signals a shift to grouping in tens. These three spoken number words conceal a crucial introduction to grouping in tens and place value in the symbolic code, which is not reflected verbally until we reach the number 'thir-teen' – even then, 'thir', a corruption of 'three', is not obviously related to 'three' and 'teen' is a corruption of 'ten'. Also, the order of the word ('thir' then 'teen'), is opposite to the order of the numeral 13, that is, 10 then 3. However, we can make a bridge between the arbitrary nature of the words 'ten', 'eleven' and 'twelve', and their the symbolic code 10, 11 and 12, by using British Sign Language (BSL) (Smith and Hodgson, 1998) and Makaton® (Makaton, 1993a,b) signs for these numbers, alongside Numicon images. For example, the manual sign for eleven in Makaton® (consisting of the signs for ten+one combined

[2] In a lecture delivered to Brighton and Hove Speech and Language Support Service in 2002; see also Grauberg (1998).

in sequence) shares a key visual and kinaesthetic link with the BSL sign for eleven (the index finger of the one from the Makaton® eleven (ten+ one) sign is the index finger that taps the thumb in the BSL sign for eleven): the Numicon 10-shape and 1-shape arranged together to represent 11 helps to explain that when we want to say 'ten-one' [sign Makaton® sign] in everyday English, we say 'eleven' [sign BSL sign for eleven].

An additional problem is that we say the names of the 'teens' numbers the 'wrong way' round, that is, in the word 'eighteen' the 'eight' comes first and is *said* first; in the numeral for '18' 'eight' is said first, but appears second. The reciting in order of names of teen numbers after twelve, breaks the normal reading-from-left-to-right rule, and the corrupted stems of thirteen and fifteen obscure their 'three' and 'five' meanings. Likewise, the stems of the words 'twenty', 'thirty', and 'fifty', 'twen-', 'thir-', 'fif-', are corruptions that obscure the 'two-', 'three-', 'five-' meanings, which would reflect the numerals in their symbolic representations. In addition, the phonological similarity between many of the words used to name numbers is confusing (e.g., 'thirteen' is phonologically different from 'thirty' by only one sound (/n/) – and, the difficulty is compounded since the nasal sound is very difficult to perceive in a noisy classroom). There are also conflicts between the names and the symbolic codes for bigger numbers, for example, 'two hundred and three' and the symbolic code '203'. Pupils often write '2003' instead of for '203' because '200 and 3' is the how we actually say it. Many pupils with difficulties learning mathematics often become exasperated with number, and these problems can impact negatively on their self-esteem, confidence and their image of themselves as learners of mathematics, leading to behavioural difficulties during mathematics lessons.

Fig 8: Putting Numicon Shapes together to show addition.

Fig 9: Showing 'take away' by hiding part of a Shape.

Fig 10: Showing 'difference in subtraction' by comparing two Shapes.

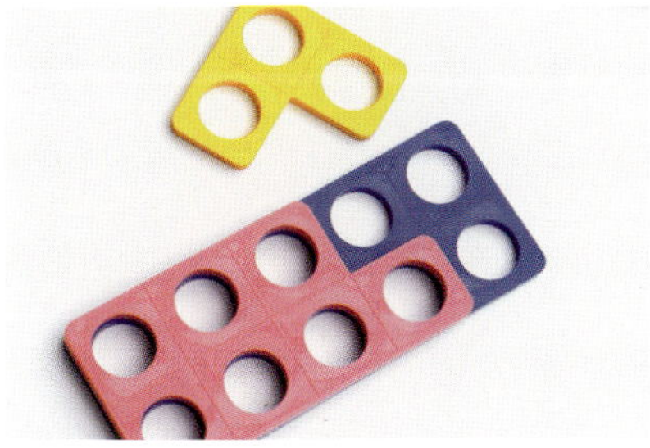

Addition

Addition has two aspects: quantities being added together, and instances of 'something more being added' (i.e., an *increase*). Generally, in introducing pupils to addition we need to introduce both aspects using appropriate language. The key words are 'together' and 'more'. Adding up prices while shopping is adding 'together', while discussing how much a pupil has grown involves 'more'. When using Numicon apparatus it is important always to represent both aspects, and to relate pupils' work with Numicon to real world situations (see figure 8).

Pupils with difficulties learning mathematics, however, may find it difficult to master different language (and processes) simultaneously when quite subtle differences of meaning both result in addition. For these pupils, it may be necessary to teach the meaning of together (with its associated mathematical process of combining sets) and, when this has been mastered, to teach the meaning of more (with its associated process of adding more objects to a pre-existing set). It may be necessary to demonstrate that the two processes produce the same result, that of 'addition'.

Subtraction

Subtraction emerges in four different situations, which is one of the reasons why pupils experience understanding (and doing) subtraction as more difficult than addition. First, there is 'take away', where there is loss (e.g., when biscuits are taken off a plate (see figure 9)). The second is 'decrease', where there is less (e.g., when the price of an object is reduced). The third is 'comparison', where there is difference (e.g., in comparing the heights of two pupils (see figure 10)). Fourthly, we have 'add on', used to check how far away a target is, which could be described as 'the inverse of addition' (e.g., how long it is to lunch time). Again, when using Numicon, all four situations must be represented and described using appropriate language. And, also, because pupils with difficulties learning mathematics often find it very difficult simultaneously to master different language (and processes) which have very similar meanings and the same results, it may be helpful to teach the names of each process, and how to undertake each process separately, as in the sequence of teaching shown on the Activity Cards. In Numicon Kit 1 it is explained that all of these processes are called subtraction.

The inverse relation between addition and subtraction

Learning linguistic terms as pairs of opposites can be challenging for pupils with language difficulties (see Section 4). Mathematically it is incorrect to think of addition and subtraction as opposites. In fact they are inverse rather than opposite processes and it is important to teach that addition and subtraction are processes of doing and undoing, that is, that they are reversible.

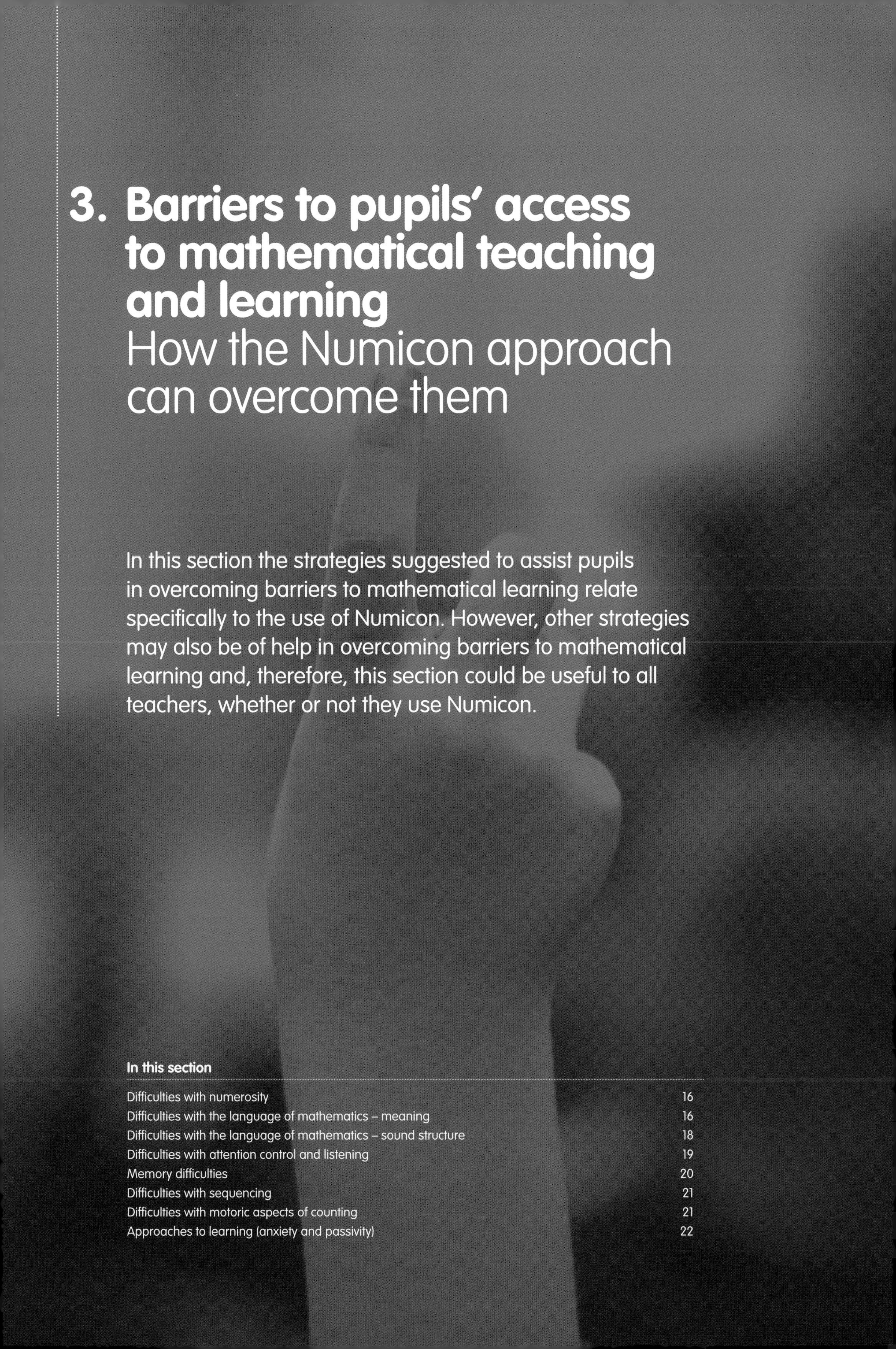

3. Barriers to pupils' access to mathematical teaching and learning
How the Numicon approach can overcome them

In this section the strategies suggested to assist pupils in overcoming barriers to mathematical learning relate specifically to the use of Numicon. However, other strategies may also be of help in overcoming barriers to mathematical learning and, therefore, this section could be useful to all teachers, whether or not they use Numicon.

In this section

Difficulties with numerosity

Pupils' development of numerosity (the size of sets) is obviously of crucial importance to their understanding of mathematics. However, pupils' other cognitive abilities and, more importantly, the way they are taught, are clearly significant if not decisive factors in the acquisition and application of arithmetic skills. There has been much debate about whether arithmetic difficulties result from deficits in pupils' awareness of numerosity, or whether these difficulties result from deficits in other cognitive areas. The typical developmental sequence for arithmetic competency is summarised by Brian Butterworth as :

- discrimination of small numerosities (the numbers of objects in sets) (from birth)
- beginning to learn the sequence of counting words and an ability to undertake 'one-to-one correspondence in sharing tasks (2 years)[1]
- the ability to add and subtract one with objects and number words, and the ability to use the cardinal principle to establish the numerosity of a set (3 years 6 months)
- the ability to add small numbers without being able to count out the sum (5 years)
- the understanding of the commutativity of addition, the ability to count on from the larger number when adding and the ability to count correctly to 40 (5 years 6 months)
- the understanding of the complementarity of addition and subtraction and the ability to count correctly to 80 (6 years 6 months)
- the retrieval of some arithmetic facts from memory (7 years). (Butterworth, 2005: 12)

The activities included in this kit take account of this progression and include many suggestions, on the Counting Activity Cards, for teaching pupils to count and encouraging them to learn the count sequence and understand the system for naming numbers. However, in pupils' work with Numicon they are able also to add numbers without counting and to see that numbers can be added together in any order, that is, that addition is commutative. When they put Numicon Shapes together in addition, and separate or compare Shapes in subtraction, they can see the inverse relation between addition and subtraction – they can see how one operation 'undoes' the other.

Difficulties with the language of mathematics – meaning

Although many pupils with verbal or spatial problems may experience difficulties with mathematics, these difficulties 'cannot be used as definite predictors of either the existence or type of mathematical difficulty that a pupil may have' (Dowker, 2004: 10). However, the language of mathematics does present specific problems for many children. Size (cardinality) and order (ordinality) of numbers, and early calculation, are taught through explanations that rely upon comprehension of spoken language, for example, concepts such as big (bigger, biggest), small (smaller, smallest) more (most), few (fewer), less (least), before, after, next, etc. The learning of mathematics depends on an accurate understanding of these concepts *in the context of number.* However, in mathematics these words are used in specific ways, which are often subtly different to their use in other contexts, both at school and at home.

The mathematical use and understanding of the concepts big/bigger/biggest and small/ smaller/ smallest are important in mathematics, this is manifest in the frequency with which we resort to their use to explain other concepts, or to discuss mathematical ideas more generally. For example, using statements such as 'the number after six is one *bigger* than six'; 'as we count forward along the number line the numbers get *bigger'*; 'the sum of four and five can't be two (in response to a pupil's mental miscalculation), it must be *bigger* than the *bigger/biggest* of the two numbers that you are adding', etc.

[1] All approximate chronological ages.

The language used to describe these concepts poses some challenges for pupils. The comparative (bigg*er*) and superlative (bigg*est*) forms change morphologically (i.e., the suffix (-*er* and -*est*) is added to the common stem and changes the meaning). Pupils with language difficulties often find it difficult to perceive and learn the subtly different meanings behind different versions of concepts that sound very similar. Moreover, whilst some concepts have absolute meanings, others have only relative meanings, which are more difficult to grasp. For example, in the set of numbers 1 to 10 the 'biggest' number is always 10, but in a set larger than 10 it is no longer the 'biggest' number. 'Bigger' number(s) can only be determined in relation to something else – so that 'bigger' numbers change as the numbers to which they are being compared change, for example, the numbers *bigger* than 5, in the set of numbers 1 to 10, are 6, 7, 8, 9 and 10, but the numbers *bigger* than 8 are only 9 and 10. For pupils with language difficulties the relative aspect of seemingly absolute yet comparative adjectives is very confusing, because other parts of speech, such as nouns, with which they are often more familiar and comfortable, have more absolute meanings: the word *banana* always refers to a yellow, sometimes squishy, long, slightly bent fruit, whether the banana is in a fruit basket or on a supermarket shelf, but the words *bigger* and *smaller* depend on the context in which an object is being described.

Moreover, it can be argued that even the positive forms – the root forms – of adjectives, such as *big* and *small*, from which the comparative and superlative forms are derived, have a comparative aspect. For example, even though it may be correct to say 'that my pencil is *small*' and 'my car [a Ford Fiesta] is *small*', the pencil and the car are not similar in size. A car is much *bigger* than a pencil even though it is a *small* car, and probably the *biggest* possible pencil would still be *smaller* than my *small* car! So in describing a car as *'small'*, small is being used as shorthand for *'small in terms of a car'*. Clearly, this relative aspect of apparently absolute adjectives makes the acquisition of these linguistic ideas very difficult. Given that it is difficult to establish exactly what is meant by an apparently simple statement that uses a seemingly absolute concept in a non-numerical context, for example, 'that is a big pencil', it follows that understanding the comparative and superlative forms of these concepts in a mathematical context, must be infinitely more intricate. A statement such as 'the sum of 6, 2 and 3 can't be 5, because the sum of two numbers must be *bigger* than the *biggest* of the three numbers that you are adding' requires a very high level of understanding of the concepts *bigger* and *biggest* in the context of number. It is not surprising, therefore, that pupils with language difficulties, who find it difficult to understand basic concepts, find the acquisition of mathematical skills very difficult.

These problems are often compounded by the different ways that particular words used in mathematics are used in social life. For example, the word *more* is generally used and understood as an imperative; requesting *more* of a desired thing ('*More* cake, mummy!'). When *more* is used mathematically ('6 is 2 *more* than 4') it has a different and much more specific meaning. And even within the domain of mathematics, there can be differences in the meanings of words when they are applied in the context of shapes and measures, and when they are used in the context of number. Words, such as *biggest* and *smallest*, are initially learnt in the context of the sizes of different objects ('that teddy is the *biggest*'). But 'show me the biggest number' requires a different understanding of *biggest*. Whilst the height and width of a doll defines, in relation to other dolls, whether it is big, bigger and/or biggest, the dimensions of a numeral (with regard to how it is written) are irrelevant. However, in a row of Numicon Shapes arranged in order from one to ten, ten is the biggest number, in terms of both its dimensions and its cardinality. When we use linguistic concepts to discuss or explain the number line we encounter similar problems: for example, in 'What are we doing *after* dinner?' 'after' is used in a temporal sense, whereas in 'Which number comes *after* 5?' the word 'after' implies position and so has a subtly different meaning.

The key visual advantage of the Numicon Shapes is their representation of the idea of the relative cardinality (value) of numbers: the Numicon Shapes clearly show that 5 is *one more* than 4 and *one less* than 6. This provides a clear visual representation of the mathematical concepts of *big (bigger, biggest), small (smaller, smallest), more (most), less (least), before, after, difference, etc.* Visual representation of these concepts using pairs or sets of Numicon Shapes, provides a bridge between pupils' social, or other understanding of these concepts, and their specific meaning in the context of number, and this is especially useful for pupils with no prior understanding of these concepts. Numicon Shapes can be used very effectively alongside alternative or augmentative communication systems, such as Makaton®, which use signs and symbols alongside speech for these basic concepts. Numicon Shapes combined with signs, symbols and spoken words, constitutes a powerful tool for pupils who have more severe learning difficulties. Their use within an augmentative and alternative communication approach will enable the inclusion of pupils who have a wide range of SEN, including pupils who have specific SLCN, and/or physical and sensory needs, as well as those who have wider cognitive difficulties (see figure 1).

Fig 1: Using Numicon Shapes to support understanding of comparative language.

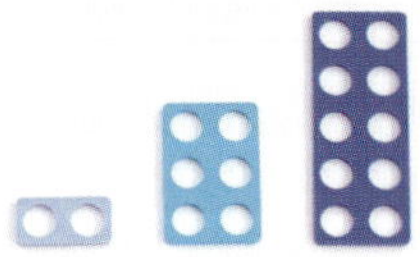

When using Numicon Shapes, it is important to consider how pairs of concepts are presented. Although it is tempting to teach these concepts through examples of opposite pairs, for a pupil who has language difficulties, using pairs of opposites may be confusing. It is simpler for the pupil to learn the meaning of one idea (e.g., big, in contrast to 'not big'), and then to learn its 'opposite' (i.e., small, in contrast to 'not small'), as separate exercises and before trying to use both concepts within a single task.

Difficulties with the language of mathematics – sound structure

Many pupils with speech and language difficulties have problems with both the sound structure (phonology) of mathematical words and with understanding their specific meanings (semantics). For example, as well as having difficulty understanding the meaning of the suffixes (morphemes) er and est, because these sound very similar, pupils with SEN may have difficulties perceiving the difference between words that incorporate them, and in storing and recalling such words accurately. Pupils with language difficulties often store in their minds 'fuzzy (phonological) representations' of concepts. For example their storage of 'big'; 'bigger' and 'biggest', as sound sequences, may be very imprecise, leading to equally imprecise separation of the different meanings associated with these representations.

Phonological issues are a critical difficulty with the learning of numbers for pupils with language difficulties. For example, not only do the numbers four, five and six have minimal differences in terms of their size and position on the number line (five is only one bigger than four, etc.), but also there are many similarities in their sound structure. Four, five and six are all words of one syllable and they all start with similar sounding unvoiced fricatives /f/ or /s/. Furthermore five and six end with similar sounds, the fricatives /v/ and /s/. The sound structure of words also causes many difficulties for pupils when they are learning about place value. For example: four, fourteen and forty have only small phonological differences, fourteen, phonologically could be the same as /four/ + /teen/ or /forty/ + /n/! Many pupils with phonological difficulties may initially perceive and store fourteen and forty as the same word. Obviously it is very difficult to learn that fourteen and forty have different meanings if your verbal signs for these meanings (the sound pattern of the words themselves) are the same.

The visual properties of Numicon support the learning of number when pupils have stored in their minds 'fuzzy' phonological (sound structure) representations of numbers. For example, whilst a pupil with language difficulties may easily confuse four, five and six because, to him or her, they sound very similar, the Numicon Shapes of these numbers are visually different. When Numicon Shapes are arranged to represent the numbers four, fourteen and forty, for example, pupils are able to see that there are clear and important differences in the structures of these numbers, even though the phonological differences between their number names is minimal (see figure 2).

Difficulties with attention control and listening

To learn mathematics, as is the case with any other area of learning, it is necessary for the pupil to be able to attend to the task at hand for a sufficient period of time and to be able to listen to the information given about the task. Achievement of attention control and listening skills follows a series of developmental stages.[2]

Fig 2: The differences in the structures of 14, 40 shown with Numicon Shapes.

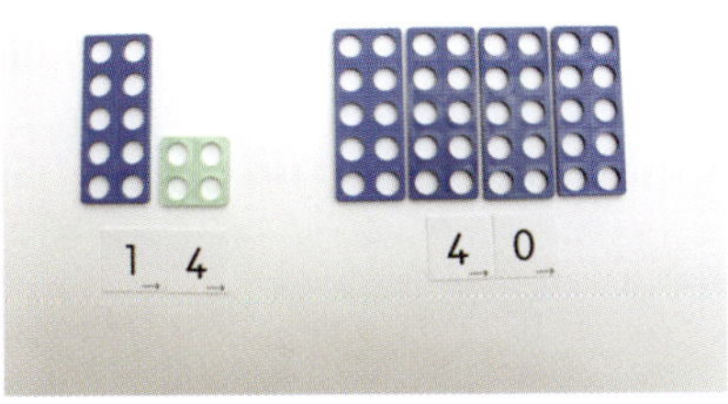

Fig 3: Pupil engaged with the practical activity of covering the Baseboard with Numicon Shapes.

Level 1 (0-1 Year) Extreme distractibility. Attention shifts from one object, person or event to another. Any new event, such as someone walking by, will immediately distract. Attention is involuntary and 'captured' by stimuli.

Level 2 (1-2 Years) Single channelled attention. Can concentrate on a concrete task of their own choosing. Cannot tolerate (ignores) verbal or visual intervention from an adult. May appear obstinate or wilful, but in fact need to ignore extraneous stimuli in order to concentrate of the task in hand. Attention still voluntary.

Level 3 (2-3 Years) Still single channelled. Cannot attend to competing auditory and visual stimuli from different sources – e.g. listening to an adult's direction while playing. But, with an adult's help, they can shift their full attention to the speaker and then back to the game.

Level 4 (3-4 Years) Still alternates full attention between the speaker and the task. Now does this spontaneously, without the adult needing to focus and re-focus that attention.

Level 5 (4-5 Years) Attention is now two channelled. The pupil understands verbal instructions related to the task without interrupting the activity to look at the speaker. Concentration span may still be short, but group instruction is possible. Moving from broad to selective pickup of information. Able to focus on a single aspect of a complex situation.

Level 6 (5-6 Years) The final stage. Auditory, visual and manipulatory channels are fully integrated. Attention is well established and maintained. Gradually able to shut out unwanted, irrelevant information and concentrate only on the essential aspects.

Pupils experiencing difficulty learning mathematics may be at an earlier stage of attention control and listening development than their chronological age would indicate and, therefore, may find it very difficult to sustain attention and to listen for the time required to understand and complete adult-directed mathematical tasks. This means that they will not learn the mathematical knowledge and skills that the tasks are designed to teach.

Pupils who have attention and listening difficulties often find tasks that involve looking and doing easier than those that require their simply listening. The Numicon teaching approach emphasises learning through action and learning by seeing, and supports attention to 'doing' tasks (see figure 3). Practical mathematical tasks with Numicon are likely to motivate and engage pupils because the Numicon Shapes make it easier for them to understand the task and to taste success, because pupils can easily self-correct when working with Numicon. However, in order to move pupils on in their thinking there must be interaction with the teacher, so their work will often be accompanied by direct verbal teaching. Those pupils whose attention level is single-channelled will not be able to do a task, and at the same time listen to verbal information; therefore, when you want

[2] Stages of Attention Control and Listening Development, available at www.cumbria.gov.uk/elibrary/Content/Internet/537/705/1109/1111/1114/37965143848.pdf, accessed 08/07/08.

to comment verbally on an aspect of a 'doing' task, you may need to ask the children to stop, and put their Numicon Shapes down on the table, before giving a visual and verbal demonstration of a particular point to the pupils. When you have done this they can then resume 'doing' with the Shapes.

Memory difficulties

We all have short term and long term memory systems,. Our short-term memory systems (auditory-verbal working memory and visual-sketchpad working memory), are used for thinking about immediate tasks, and our long-term memory systems (semantic, visual-spatial, procedural (motor) and episodic memory), are used to store and recall information (Bristow et al. 1999). Pupils with language and/or learning difficulties often have stronger visual-sketchpad, visual-spatial and procedural (motor) memory systems (which use shape, space and actions) than auditory-verbal and semantic memories (which use mostly sound sequences and word meanings). The teaching of mathematics often relies on the use of verbal explanations and rote verbal counting, and poses verbal problems without structured visual support; therefore this tends to be very demanding of the weaker auditory-verbal and semantic memory systems of pupils with language and/or learning difficulties, whereas the use of pattern, shape, space and motor actions utilises pupils' stronger visual motor memory systems.

The Numicon Shapes, which give a clear visual structured representation for each number, allow pupils to use their visual-sketchpad short term memory and their visual-spatial long term memory to help them process and remember the names and relative sizes of numbers and, later, addition and subtraction facts as well. It is often easier for a pupil with working memory difficulties to hold the Numicon Shapes in their visual-sketchpad memories than it is for them to hold the sound of the number names in their auditory-verbal working memories. The Numicon Shapes can be held in the pupil's long term visual-spatial memory and, in association with the names of the numbers they represent, will support the retention of the meaning of the numbers' names (their cardinal size) in the long term semantic memory. Consequently, many pupils who may have experienced difficulty in remembering the names and cardinal sizes of numbers, and addition and subtraction facts for the numbers to ten, will find that using the Numicon Shapes makes this much easier.

Once pupils are able to associate number names with the Numicon Shapes they should be encouraged to 'see' the patterns 'in their heads'. While visualisation is often a key aspect of developing understanding and recall of ideas with pupils with language and/ or learning difficulties, it may not be something that the pupil instinctively knows how to do and they may need to be taught. It is important, therefore, to teach the pupils how to visualise. It may be necessary, for example, to show the pupils a Numicon Shape or combination of Shapes, then cover them, and ask whether they can see a picture of them in their heads (and perhaps try to draw it). Activities that involve pupils 'feeling' for the correct shape in the Feely Bag will help pupils to develop their own mental imagery, which can be recalled for solving mental arithmetic problems.

Difficulties with sequencing

Knowing the order of numbers is of critical importance to counting and calculation. However, pupils with SENs may have wider difficulties with sequencing that will make it difficult for them to learn counting and calculation. Whilst pupils' difficulties with sequencing are often apparent in their problems with learning temporal language, such as 'before' and 'after', which are used in mathematical sequences, their difficulties with sequencing and organisation may go wider than temporal language alone. For example, if you are not sure what the sequence of your day is, let alone how this sequence is described with temporal concepts, then learning that '5 comes after 6' is likely to be extremely challenging. It is necessary to know the sequence of a day's activities – for instance the relative order of the register, the maths lesson, playtime, snack time, the literacy lesson, lunch time, etc. – in order to be able to map language such as 'we'll have our snack *after* playtime' to the sequence of the day's activities and, eventually, to learn the meaning of the concept *after* in this context. It is likely that understanding the use of the concept *after* in sentences such as 'we're having our snack after break' is a prerequisite to the related, but different, use of *after* in statements such as '6 is the number that comes after 5' on the number line (see figure 4).

Fig 4: Supporting understanding of temporal concepts through the use of visual timetables.

Fig 5: Pupil engaged in putting the Numicon Shapes into order.

The visual properties of Numicon, its step-like size increase from one number to the next, allow pupils to see and thus understand visually the relative positions of numbers in sequence (see figure 5). Instead of a number sequence appearing to be an arbitrary series of sounds (number names) or symbols (numerals), the reason for each number's place in the number sequence can be *seen*. For example, with Numicon images, five is visually *one more/bigger than* four and *one less/smaller than* six: the order of four, five and six is shown through the relative sizes of the Numicon Shapes. Seeing and manipulating Numicon Shapes into order, helps pupils to develop an understanding of relationships between number and number sequences, which is essential to successful counting and calculation.

Difficulties with motoric aspects of counting

For many pupils learning the temporal use of concepts, such as *before* and *after*, is built upon experience and understanding of gross and fine motor sequences (such as moving left to right along repeating patterns) and visual sequences (such as visual patterns and pictorial/symbolic visual timetables). Therefore, for pupils with SEN who have difficulties in performing the fine, gross and oral movements in time and space that are necessary for the motor execution of sequences such as counting, the difficulties with the cognitive aspects of sequencing are compounded. For example, it is very difficult to count a set of objects accurately if you do not have firm knowledge of the sequence (order) of numbers, and this difficulty is compounded if you also find it difficult to co-ordinate the fine motor skills needed to move your finger from one object to the next, with the oral motor skills needed to say the numbers in the count.

Wherever possible, pupils should be encouraged wherever possible to connect their counting with number lines so that they connect the size of the count to the place of the last number in the count on the number line. However, it is important to remember that the fine motor skills required to count sets of small objects and to use small number lines is a refinement of gross motor counting. Pupils with fine motor difficulties need to count using larger motor movements before they learn to localise the motoric aspect of counting in a fine motor count. The size of the Numicon Shapes, the possibility of varying the distances between them when spacing them out in sequence and their robustness, enables counting activities to be adapted to take account of the precision of pupils' motor movements. Some pupils may count along a Numicon Large Format Table Top Number Line; other pupils, with less refined motor skills, may need Numicon Shapes to be spaced out in sequence on a table top to create a number line along which they can count using large motor movements. Others may need to move their whole bodies along a number line of Numicon Shapes placed on the floor before they learn to localise the motoric aspect of counting (see figure 6 & 7).

Approaches to learning (anxiety and passivity)

Pupils' approaches to learning – which may result from within-pupil factors, social factors or previous experience of teaching and learning mathematics in school – have a significant impact on their acquisition of mathematical skills. To prevent anxiety developing about mathematics, which is less common in younger pupils than older students, early intervention in the form of appropriate teaching is recommended. The activities in this kit should benefit older pupils who may be experiencing considerable anxiety in undertaking mathematical tasks. Whilst success with mathematics, which this kit aims to facilitate, will obviously be a key factor in overcoming anxiety, some pupils may need additional emotional support during their learning of mathematics to address this anxiety and to promote greater engagement with mathematical learning.

Passivity in a learning situation is a great concern, and will often result in little of the hoped for learning happening. Pupils who have experienced repeated failure will often seek to avoid further pain by non-participation. Also, some pupils, with some types of SEN, may have particularly passive learning styles. The opportunities suggested by Numicon for simple physical action, which can be experimental and also self-correcting, may entice some pupils into physical engagement that will lead to thinking.

Fig 6: Counting along a large scale Numicon Number Line made with 'mats'.

Fig 7: Jumping along a large scale Numicon Number Line.

4. **Using and applying mathematics** – including functioning in the wider world

Planning to teach mathematics in a way that supports the acquisition of independent life skills is important, and particularly for pupils who have more severe learning difficulties because, for them, a significant part of the curriculum will be focused upon acquiring life skills.

In this section

This Closing the Gap Teaching Programme aims to establish a firm foundation for basic number understanding and skills that underpin everyday mathematical functioning. These skills are developed further in subsequent Numicon kits. All pupils should be encouraged to apply their growing competency to solving mathematical problems and to everyday life situations. Practising teachers in the United Kingdom are expected to encourage their pupils to apply their mathematics by posing them mathematical word problems; however, for some pupils it may be easier and more motivating to learn mathematical competencies within the context of life skills in real and meaningful situations, because they can immediately see the relevance to their everyday lives of what they are learning. Therefore it is recommended that pupils have ample opportunities to use and apply their growing understanding in problems that are relevant to them. All the Numicon activities are under continuous review and as such are work in progress and, thus, further work on developing such a problem solving approach is underway.[1]

Skills learning has been described as a four (or five) step process in 'The Instructional Hierarchy': acquisition, fluency, (maintenance), generalisation and adaptation (Haring et al. 1978).[2] Figure 1 depicts these steps in a mathematics context involving the learning and application of number facts and calculation.

We have adapted the model to include generalising *and* transferring, both of which are central aspects of mathematical thinking: *generalising* is the ability *to make general statements* (e.g. 4 + 5 = 9 is a general statement about all situations in which 4 of something and 5 of something are added) and *transferring* is the ability to *transfer skills and knowledge from one situation to another* (e.g., transferring the knowledge that 4 sweets and 5 sweets combine to make 9 sweets, to know that combining 4 football cards and 5 football cards will yield 9 football cards). The generalisation and *adaptation stages* of the model are often referred to in mathematics as 'using and applying'. These stages are not represented in the more usual linear form, to reflect that the acquisition of mathematical skills should be related to the real world in the first place – and that it is neither easy, nor necessarily desirable, to divorce acquisition from generalisation, in the mathematical sense.

Teaching approaches which support the stages learning model and help pupils overcome difficulties with using and applying their mathematical understanding

Throughout the Teaching Programme there is much repetition to support acquisition, fluency and maintenance of number facts. The teaching activities support mathematical thinking and the progression within the Teaching Programme means that pupils are consistently required to use prior knowledge and see its relevance to new situations. It is important also to encourage pupils to transfer and adapt their mathematical knowledge and skills to the ultimate goal of using their mathematical competencies spontaneously in novel tasks and everyday situations. Within each teaching session connections should be made to help pupils to use and apply their understanding, including real life situations such as cooking, shopping, going on the bus, etc., some of which can be acted out in

[1] This means that the distinction between 'acquisition' and 'generalisation' in the model in Figure 1 is not always clear-cut: for some children and young people the 'acquisition' of mathematical competence occurs within learning contexts in which the acquisition of mathematical competencies is embedded in (or 'generalised' from) real world situations.

[2] Haring et al. identify four stages: acquisition, fluency, generalisation and adaptation. Our inclusion of a 'maintenance' stage (also included by other writers) in our use of this model emphasises the need for children and young people experiencing difficulties learning mathematics to over learn and revisit skills, in order to maintain fluency.

Acquisition

The initial teaching/learning of the skills required to calculate 4 + 5. The initial teaching/learning of the number fact 4 + 5 = 9.

This might be taught with Numicon Shapes 4, 5, 9; or in an applied context, e.g. '4 sweets and 5 sweets making 9 sweets altogether' in a role-play shop; or using Numicon Shapes to help pupils understand the applied context. Whatever the initial teaching situation might be, pupils have to generalise eventually the general rule that the sum of 4 and 5 anythings will always be 9.

Adaptation

The ability to recognise that knowing the fact 4 + 5 = 9 can help you to calculate/predict the sum of 40 + 50

Fluency

The ability consistently to calculate 4 + 5. The ability to remember consistently that 4 + 5 = 9

4 + 5 = 9

Generalisation

Generalising: Recognising the general rule that the sum of 4 and 5 is always 9, and

Transferring: The ability to transfer the calculating skill and memory that 4 + 5 = 9 to solve problems like, 'If you had four football cards, and your friend gave you another five, then how many cards would you have to trade in the playground?'

Maintenance

The ability to remember the skills required to calculate 4 + 5 (and the ability to retain that 4 + 5 = 9) even when this is not the current focus of the mathematics teaching/learning.

role play, and in other situations that are of interest and relevance to individual pupils and therefore engaging.

Pupils with difficulties learning mathematics may find the application of mathematical skills and knowledge challenging for two reasons: firstly in-child learning factors, such as linguistic competence, and secondly, how the mathematics has been taught. For example, a pupil who knows that 4 + 5 = 9 may not be able to answer the question 'if you had four football cards, and your friend gave you another five, then how many cards would you have to trade in the playground'?[3] either because s/he may not understand the language of the question or/and s/he has had no experience of applying mathematical competencies in word problems like this in maths lessons.
These in-child learning factors include:

- difficulty with short term auditory-verbal working memory making it difficult for the pupil to hold the sentence describing the mathematical problem long enough to process its meaning;
- difficulty understanding the vocabulary;
- difficulty understanding grammatical structure (e.g., an if… then… structure);
- difficulty separating out the information required to solve the mathematical problem – that is, the numbers, and the specific language used to trigger a mathematical operation – from the background information. (In the football cards example, the mention of football cards may trigger other thoughts and feelings than those related to the maths required to solve the problem);
- difficulty identifying the appropriate mathematical process (addition, subtraction, etc.);
- difficulty doing the actual mathematics (e.g., recalling the number fact or performing the calculation).

To enable pupils to solve verbally expressed mathematical problems embedded in real life contexts, some pre-teaching of competencies (other than those required purely for number and calculation) may be necessary. The following strategies are suggested to help pupils apply mathematics in (verbal) problem solving situations.

- Teaching short term memory strategies, such as verbal rehearsal and visualisation, and prompting their use through such questions as: *When you listen to the maths problem what are you going to do to help you remember it? You could hold the key numbers and words in your head. You could make a picture of the maths problem in your head. You could make notes in words or pictures in your maths book. You could make a picture with Numicon Shapes in your head.* [4]
- Explaining the meaning of the vocabulary used in mathematics problems, especially words that trigger the particular mathematical process needed, for example, *'When you hear "altogether" in a maths problem it usually means that you need to add'.*

[3] Whether being able to solve a mathematical problem such as this is key to functioning in the everyday world is a moot point, but often activities embedded within the child's social context are key aspects of self esteem building and the acquisition of social kudos within a peer group. Having good self esteem and feeling part of a group are essential pre-requisites to maintaining enthusiasm for learning in school, especially if a child or young person finds learning challenging. Therefore, being able to solve this problem may be of great importance to the educational career of a child or young person and, ultimately, to their ability to function independently in adult life.

[4] Some pupils may benefit further from having Numicon Shapes printed on small cards, or having a mini Numicon number line which they can carry in their pockets and use as an aide memoire in everyday situations. Such prompts may be helpful when pupils are meeting new word problems, or problem-solving in role play at school.

- Explaining the grammatical structures commonly used in mathematical problems, for example. *'When you hear the words "if" and "then" in a maths problem, the words after "if" normally give you information that you need to remember and the words after "then" tell you what you need to do with that information'.*
- Teaching self-monitoring and self-help strategies that will enable pupils to feel sufficiently confident to ask for help with a problem solving task if they do not understand it. The most basic form of self-monitoring is for the pupil, in responding to a question, to say he or she does not know the answer, or has forgotten the question, rather than guessing at it. While informed guessing can be a useful strategy in some situations (and is essential in predicting), random guesses may obscure the pupil's real difficulties and result in no further clarification or support.[5]
- Pre-teaching pupils how to separate 'important information' from 'not important information', in the context of the specific task at hand, so that they are aware that not everything in a mathematical problem's language may be of equal importance.

The strategies listed below, in addition to those suggested above, could be used as a model for helping pupils to use and apply their mathematical skills and knowledge in lessons.

- Create opportunities for pupils to use and apply their mathematics.
- Monitor pupils' levels of comprehension during a mathematical task, clarifying the meaning of key words, and/or modifying the grammatical construction of the question.
- Remind children of the self help strategies they can use – including memory strategies and using Numicon Shapes. Prompt the use of self-monitoring and self-help strategies during problem solving tasks as necessary.
- Remind pupils to identify the important information, that is, the numbers and the mathematical process required, by *emphasising* these; for example, by signing them and/or asking the pupils to hold up or visualise the appropriate Numicon Shapes, or to jot down the numbers and the key words about the required operation as they hear them.
- Consider whether to present the problem in writing as well as verbally. It should not be assumed that all pupils with verbal language difficulties have difficulties with text decoding when reading. Some pupils with specific language difficulties are good text decoders, even though they have difficulties in understanding the meaning of what they read. For these pupils their text decoding competence can be used to support their understanding of the key mathematical components in a 'verbal' maths problem: they can, for instance, highlight the numerals and the key mathematical process words in the text. Presenting the task in writing overcomes the auditory memory load of such tasks, as a written text can be referred to as many times as necessary.
- Pupils who would benefit from a visual representation of a 'verbal' maths problem, but who find text decoding difficult may be helped by having the text of a problem presented in both words and symbols. Information technology (IT) packages, such as Widgit's *Writing with Symbols 2000*,[6] allow texts to be quickly supported by symbols, enhancing both their readability and meaning.

[5] Refer to page 37 in Teaching Approaches, for further guidance on self-monitoring
[6] see www.widgit.com/products/wws2000/index.htm

- If appropriate, when helping pupils to solve a word problem that is set in a social situation try acting out the social situation in which the mathematics problem arises and 'freeze framing' the action at crucial points, to allow the pupils to identify the numbers involved or the calculation required to solve the problem.
- Connect with Numicon Shapes. Ask pupils to arrange objects that are involved in the problem into the appropriate Numicon patterns. For the football cards example, pupils could be given actual football cards, and asked to arrange 4 and 5 cards into the Numicon patterns for these numbers, and/or
- whilst the problem is being spoken, ask the pupils to pick up the appropriate Numicon Shapes for the numbers being mentioned in the problem.

Essential life skills

In order to function independently with money and measures (length, weight, capacity, time) pupils will need to achieve the level of number understanding covered in the Numicon Kit 2 activities, which is broadly commensurate with Level 3 in the English National Curriculum. This may involve embedding the initial acquisition of mathematical competencies within everyday situations, or initially teaching specific competencies discretely, followed by a carefully planned series of activities to demonstrate their application in everyday situations. Connections will need to be explicit, otherwise pupils may be unable, for example, to add up the prices of the items they are purchasing despite having the mathematical competency to do so. The distinction between competency and functioning is crucial: competency in mathematics should enable functioning; it if does not it is of no real value.

Many basic everyday functions involve mathematical competence, for example:

- Personal organisation requires competency with time;
- Shopping requires competency with money, weight and capacity;
- Travelling by public transport requires competency with time and money;
- Social situations, such as meeting a friend at a café, require competency with time and money.

Situations that require personal, social, health and citizenship knowledge, skills and understanding will require situation specific competencies. For example:

- healthy eating requires competency with weight, capacity and time;
- going to see the doctor and taking medication requires competency with time, money and capacity.

At the time of writing, comprehensive activities using Numicon to teach older pupils the mathematical skills required for everyday life are still being developed; however, below we provide outline suggestions for in using Numicon in the key aspects of measurement (including time) and money.

Time

Competency with time is important for personal organisation (e.g., being in the right place at the right time; knowing what time to get up; having with you all the things you need); for travelling (e.g., knowing what time to catch the bus); social situations (e.g., when you are meeting a friend at a café); staying healthy (making appointments with the dentist, doctor, hairdresser, and so on). Although some degree of competency with telling the time can be achieved using a digital clock (and this might be the goal for some pupils), learning to tell the time with full competency involves:

- understanding of linguist time concepts (e.g., before, after, etc.)
- understanding ('feel') of the duration of units of time (second, minute, hour)
- ability to tell the time (read a clock)
- ability to perform calculations using time (e.g., relating cooking instructions, such as ' heat for 12 minutes', to the time on the clock).

Numicon Shapes can be used to support teaching pupils to tell the time in the following ways:

- Supporting understanding of the numerals on the clock face by arranging Numicon Shapes around the perimeter.
- Developing multiplication skills: pupils meet the number ideas required for telling the time in Numicon Kit 2 when multiplication is introduced and pupils can relate this to counting in 5s around the five minute divisions on the clock face and relate multiplying by 10 to counting in 10s, and the passage of time.
- Developing fraction knowledge: also in the work in Numicon Kit 2 pupils are introduced to fractions – and learn to use the words half and quarter in relation to number ideas.

Money

Competency with money is important for many aspects of independent living – the most obvious of which being shopping; but also socialising – buying cinema tickets, buying a coffee for a friend; travelling – paying fares; and, crucially, for avoiding exploitation by knowing how much change should be received, knowing whether utility bills are correct; knowing that wages are correct, etc. Adults who are innumerate simply have to trust the honesty of those they encounter in all situations where money transactions are involved. Full competency with money involves understanding of equivalence, place value and calculation and the ability to transfer and generalise this understanding. At a basic functional level competency with money requires:

- ability to recognise coins;
- understanding the relative value of coins (e.g., that a 5p coin is of equivalent value to five 1p coins, etc.);
- ability to perform calculations using coins;
- ability to understand money-specific language (e.g., 'change', how much money do you need [meaning how many 1p/£1 units], 'too much/expensive', 'not enough' etc.);

Numicon Shapes can be used to help pupils develop competency with money in various ways:

- making connections between the relative values of the Numicon Shapes and relative values of coins by affixing coins to the corresponding Numicon Shapes – this is explained in Kit 1;
- calculating with low value coins is introduced in Numicon Kit 1 and is extended to include calculating to pounds and pence in Numicon Kit 2;
- when pupils are using money to shop, provide them with a small 'memory jogger card' that has pictures of coins linked to Numicon Shapes.

Measures of length, weight and capacity

The ability to measure length, weight and capacity is essential for many aspects of everyday life and is often a requirement for employment. Pupils need to develop a true understanding of these standard measures, and will do so only through repeated practical activities, which give them opportunities to experience and 'feel' the value of these standard measures. Full competency with measures involves understanding of place value, equivalence and calculations involving four digit numbers, and the ability to transfer and generalise this understanding. At a functional level competency with measures requires:

- understanding the concepts and comparative language associated with measures. In the context of length, long/er/est; short/er/est narrow/er/est etc.; in the context of weight, heavy/ier/iest and light/er/est; in the context of capacity, full, half full, half empty, empty, etc.),
- understanding ('feel') of the value of units of weight (kilograms, grams/stones, pounds, ounces), capacity (millilitres, litres/fluid ounces, pints) and length (kilometres, metres, centimetres, millimetres/miles, feet, inches),
- ability to perform calculations using weight and capacity measures.

For pupils who have language difficulties it is useful to link current learning to previous learning. When pupils are being taught 'heavier' and 'lighter' a link could be made to 'bigger' and 'smaller' (e.g. 'heavier' is a 'bigger' amount of weight, and 'lighter' a 'smaller'),[7] and perhaps illustrated by providing a visual analogy where relative values of different measured amounts are represented by Numicon Shapes. For instance, in cooking activities two tablespoonfuls of flour could be linked to the Numicon 2-shape. Later, the weight/capacity of amounts could be measured and represented with Numicon Shapes to explain, for instance, that the number of kilograms in 10kg is *bigger* than the number of kilograms in 5kg (with the Numicon representations of 10 and 5); therefore, we can say that 10kg is *heavier* (or a *bigger weight*).

[7] Wendy Rinaldi discusses the hierarchical nature of concept acquisition in Rinaldi (2005), which contains some useful guidance on the teaching of mathematical concepts.

5. Teaching Approaches and Organisation – General Guidance

The Closing the Gap with Numicon Teaching Activities are designed both for use in short term intervention programmes, and also for teaching children who have SEN who are likely to require long term support. Both these groups of pupils are likely to be working in one-to-one or in small group situations. There are no absolute rules about grouping to teach Numicon activities; recent research on using Numicon in short-term intervention programmes has shown a combination of one-to-one teaching and small group work, involving two or three pupils, to be successful; whilst other projects where pupils have only worked in small groups have also been effective.

In this section

Including all pupils

The adage that 'what is good teaching for pupils with SEN is good teaching for all', although an oversimplification, is generally true. Numicon Shapes and Number Rods can be used to support all levels of learning, including that of the most able pupils aged 11 and over. Problem solving challenges are currently being developed (see the Numicon website www.numicon.com for developments). It is important that there is no perception within the class that Numicon is used only by pupils of 'lower ability', which would make it a stigmatising rather than a change agent. If one group of pupils is working with Numicon to develop basic mathematical skills, whenever possible, other groups of pupils should be using, for example, Numicon Rods and other tangible mathematical apparatus, to develop more complex mathematical skills, concepts and knowledge.

Similarly, signs and symbols are not applicable only to pupils with learning difficulties; their use is helpful for all pupils being introduced to a new mathematical concept. Also, it is important that the signing of key concepts applies to the whole class, which will avoid any stigmatising of lower attaining students. For the latter the signing will be of immense help in pointing out the important concepts; other pupils will be able to focus upon the more complex vocabulary whether or not it is signed.

Creating a mathematics learning environment for all pupils

Whilst maths underpins so many aspects of our lives, the visual profile of maths and numbers is often low, so many pupils do not see maths as being relevant, which can have a potentially negative effect on their attitude to learning the subject. Therefore, in the same way that pupils should be immersed in differentiated and targeted language *that supports their language learning,* they need to be immersed in a visually rich mathematical environment *that supports their learning of mathematics.* Most pupils notice and take in their surroundings making much of their learning 'opportunistic'; so, a designated maths area can stimulate thinking about mathematical ideas and pupils can be helped to use it independently, for instance, by labelling drawers and containers, using signs that incorporate numerals, pictures and words (and perhaps with Makaton® or Rebus symbols).[1] The Numicon number line, displayed at pupil eye level so that they can refer to it easily while working, should be a key feature of a maths area. At the same time, teachers must be aware and wary of 'visual overload': in the same way that pupils who have difficulties learning mathematics can be confused through linguistic overload, they can be equally confused by visual overload. So whilst it is important to provide a number rich environment, for example, by including numerals in notices to say how many pupils may work on the computer at one time, it is equally important to ensure that the visual environment *supports the ongoing mathematical learning objectives.* For instance, if the most prominent feature of a pupil's mathematical visual environment is a number line to 1,000, with no representation of 1 to 10, this will not help him or her to group, count, read or write numbers up to 10.

Maths displays are useful to reinforce the current teaching focus, and might include various activities around a theme. They should be engaging and attractive and could include a mix of two dimensional and three dimensional images, perhaps going up and down the wall as well as along the wall, table or shelf. Examples of pupils' work could be included, which the pupils themselves could arrange. The key information should be free of extraneous information (linguistic clutter) and free of unnecessary

[1] Symbols can be generated for use on labels, and for teaching key concepts, using IT resources such as Widget Software's Writing with Symbols, see www.widgit.com/products/wws2000/index.htm, accessed 8.07.08.

physical clutter (the pupils should be encouraged to keep it tidy). Any numerals included in the display should be in a clear font (or handwriting style) and of a size that is suitable for pupils with visual impairments. Similarly, care should be taken over the tonal variation between the text and the background. Pupils quickly accept a display as part of the classroom landscape; it is important to keep displays fresh and interesting whilst maintaining number lines as a constant feature on which pupils can depend.

Some children who experience difficulties learning mathematics (or who have other learning or organisational difficulties, visual impairments, semantic-pragmatic language difficulties or/and ASC) may not be able to process their visual environment in an organised manner: what may be meant to be the most important idea in a display, may not be obvious to pupils with difficulties. For example, pupils with semantic-pragmatic language disorder, ASC, and some visual impairments, may find it extremely difficult, cognitively or visually, to differentiate a figure or object (the most important information) from the ground (the background information). This occurs particularly when displays are so 'busy' as to result in sensory/perceptual overload. Some pupils who have SEN may rarely attend to their visual environment and they may need to be taught how to look at particular aspects of a display and shown how to use them to support their learning of targeted mathematical skills, knowledge and understanding. If displays are used, they must have aspects that support current learning, otherwise they are not useful.

It is important to remember that pupils with ASC sometimes find very stimulating visual displays result in sensory overload, causing raised anxiety levels, 'shutting down' and/or challenging behaviour. Pupils who have severe ASC who experience sensory-perceptual difficulties may find it easier to work just with the equipment, in an environment with no potentially distracting additions. In a mainstream context this does not mean working in an environment with no displays, but rather thinking about where you will teach such a pupil to enable him or her to focus on a particular learning intention; the busy classroom may not the best place. You may need to control the amount of sensory information in the equipment: for instance, a pupil who has ASC may be more interested in (and distracted by) the colour of the Numicon images than their relative size. As the most important part of the pieces is their relative size it maybe necessary to work with photocopied, black and white, cut out images.

Encouraging positive attitudes to learning maths

Using Numicon generally increases pupils' confidence. They are usually fascinated by the relationships they can see between the Shapes, and the combinations they can make with them. Pupils that have progressed to Key Stage 2 and above – and especially those in mainstream contexts, and who have experienced repeated failure with mathematical learning, should be encouraged to use Numicon. Pupils' attitudes to Numicon will depend heavily on how its use is introduced, and for some older pupils it may be necessary to re-label activities 'visual problem solving', or 'discovery challenge', for example, rather than 'play' to avoid any association between 'play' in the classroom, and childishness and/or 'being stupid'. The relationships and combinations encountered when using the kit give pupils insight into abstract ideas about numbers and arithmetic. Where previously pupils perhaps had to rely on counting to learn number facts 6 + 4 = 10, with Numicon Shapes they can see the fact and *know* that it is true and this knowledge gives them confidence. They can also use the patterns of the Numicon Shapes to make predictions about number in much the same way as they use pictures when learning to read. The visual structure and practical, self-correcting nature of the activities mean that pupils are willing to experiment with ideas whilst their engagement in and enjoyment of the Activities will promote their long term memory of the learning. Teachers are enabled to recognise where pupils have a lack of understanding or confusion and to provide effective intervention. Sharing in pupils' discoveries and praising their efforts will also help to make the experience positive for teachers and pupils.

Grouping pupils

The Closing the Gap with Numicon Teaching Activities are designed both for use in short term intervention programmes, and also for teaching children who have SEN who are likely to require long term support. Both these groups of pupils are likely to be working in one-to-one or in small group situations. There are no absolute rules about grouping to teach Numicon activities; recent research on using Numicon in short-term intervention programmes has shown a combination of one-to-one teaching and small group work, involving two or three pupils, to be successful; whilst other projects where pupils have only worked in small groups have also been effective.[2] In either case the focus in the organisation of teaching must be on developing and maintaining the self-esteem and self-concept as mathematical learners of pupils who have difficulties learning mathematics. Pupils will learn at the optimal level only if they feel confident as mathematical learners. To achieve this, we need to consider certain factors.

It is recommended that pupils with mathematical difficulties, at Key Stage 2 and above, who are working at P Levels, or National Curriculum (for England) Levels 1 or 2, should be taught number skills in ability-based groups. This should not preclude their learning with more mathematically able pupils at other times in the school week – it is important for them to experience the comments and conversations of more mathematically able learners (unless this is detrimental to their self-esteem as mathematical learners).

Where possible, small group number teaching sessions using Numicon, should take place within the daily mathematics lesson, as one of the adult-supported group activities. The suggested Teaching Activities link more closely to the early years foundation stage and Key Stage 1 mathematics teaching objectives for number, than to Key Stage 2 objectives. However, best practice differentiation entails the teaching of the same broad mathematical objectives, but at the level determined by the pupil's needs: for instance, if the learning intention for the lesson is 'Counting and ordering numbers to 1,000' then it would be appropriate for a group of pupils with SEN to be undertaking work counting and ordering numbers to 10. If this work were undertaken within the whole class (assuming that the learning environment – noise level, behaviour, etc. – was conducive to learning), this would likely enhance the pupils' self-esteem and self-concept as mathematically competent learners.

The Numicon Teaching Programme addresses the number and calculation aspects of the mathematics curriculum, and it is important to ensure that all pupils also receive their entitlement to the Shape, Space and Measures aspects. Therefore, if the whole class learning intention relates to Shape, Space and Measures, the pupils in the Numicon group must not miss out and the Numicon number activities must be undertaken at another time, and not within the normal mathematics lesson; this involves some attention to timetabling. It is important also to maintain curriculum balance; pupils withdrawn to do Numicon number work at a time other than during daily mathematics lesson, must be given the opportunity to experience the parts of the curriculum that they are missing as a result.

On occasion, even though the objectives of the whole-class mathematics lesson relate to number, it is better to withdraw pupils to undertake Numicon number activities. For example, if the environment of the classroom is not conducive to the learning needs

[2] Refer to the Numicon website www.numicon.com for details of independent research projects.

of pupils who have SEN – if the whole class environment is noisy or over sensorily stimulating. There is considerable evidence that the noise level in the classroom has a significant impact upon the ability of pupils with SEN to pick out the figure (the sounds of speech) from the ground (the background noise of the classroom), making it very difficult for them to attend to the language of instruction. If the level of noise in the classroom makes it difficult for a group of pupils with SEN to learn, it is probably making it difficult for many other pupils. Therefore, it is important to control the noise level in the room. Nevertheless, for some pupils who have SEN, and especially those with ASD, the classroom can be over-stimulating, making it difficult for them to attend to the mathematical learning objectives that are the focus.

Another reason for withdrawing SEN pupils is when the mathematical activities being undertaken by the whole class are so vastly different from the work being done by the small group that the group learning is perceived by the pupils with difficulties as stigmatising. Attention needs to be given to the aspects of teaching that underline similarity rather than difference. For example, if the group of pupils with difficulties learning mathematics is the only group using materials/apparatus, there can be a perception that use of materials and learning difficulties are connected. Any association between using Numicon and being less able must be avoided. This can be achieved in part, by ensuring that the whole class is using tangible materials in their learning, including Numicon Shapes and Number Rods. Those conducting intervention programmes report that pupils benefit where a similar teaching approach is used for the whole class and the withdrawal sessions for one to one or small group teaching, that is, for both to use Numicon.

Planning and structuring teaching sessions with Numicon

It is helpful to check out the key mathematical ideas behind the chosen Teaching Activity (found in section 2 of this Teaching Guide), as understanding the point of the activity will help you to anticipate the areas of pupils' likely difficulties and give you the confidence to improvise when they ask questions and respond in ways you had not foreseen. Trying out the activities yourselves helps you to identify which aspects the pupils might find difficult, and you can then refer to the strategies recommended in this Teaching Guide for overcoming potential barriers to learning. For some pupils it may be that an activity requires further modification. The following are examples of modifications that can be planned prior to teaching, or implemented after evaluating a pupil's response to your initial teaching:

- spending more or less time on certain activities than originally anticipated;
- teaching with the recommended signs or using symbols rather than signs;
- using other visual models or images, such as Number Rods, as the primary support for the acquisition of number;
- using Numicon Interactive Whiteboard Software on a PC so pupils can 'manipulate' Numicon Shapes and Number Rods on screen;

It is important to plan carefully which vocabulary and language structures you will use in the activity noting the language of instruction as well as the mathematical language and always bearing in mind the pupils' level of language understanding. Often mathematical concepts are more easily understood if signs and/or symbols and reference to Numicon Shapes and Number Lines accompany verbal explanations.

The organisational difficulties that many pupils with SEN experience impact on their mathematical learning. This needs to be borne in mind when planning and organising small group work. Some pupils with SEN perseverate, that is, they continue thinking and talking about the previous topic area when the teaching has moved on. To develop pupils' organisation and discourage perseveration, it is useful to use a visual timetable that represents each part of the group session by a picture or symbol (e.g., Makaton®, Rebus or Picture Communication System (PCS) symbols). These timetables can be constructed quickly and simply using IT packages such as *Writing With Symbols 2000.*[3] The symbols used might be: 'finding the same shape'; 'counting forwards to 10', etc., and would clearly remind pupils about the learning objectives for each part of the session and give the teacher a framework for explaining to pupils what will be happening in the lesson.

It is recommended that teaching sessions should last approximately 25 minutes, be well paced and follow a similar structure.

Warm up Many pupils with SEN have listening and attention control difficulties, so it is useful, at the beginning of a small group session, to do a short listening and attention 'warm up'. This might take the form of a short looking and listening game. (Useful examples can be found in Rinaldi, 2005). Alternatively, the warm up could be a familiar and favourite Numicon activity such as putting the Numicon Shapes in order or Covering the Board.

Counting activity Counting is important daily practice for all pupils working towards acquiring basic number understanding. Advice on counting is given in the key mathematical ideas section 2 of this guide and ideas for counting activities are explained fully in the Programme of Teaching Activities.

Main teaching activity This will be taken from the Programme of Teaching Activities, which should be followed sequentially, or might be work on Pattern following suggestions for ideas from the Pattern Activities in the Programme.

Application Helping pupils to use and apply what they have learnt to real world contexts is an essential element of their mathematics learning. This will involve posing problems for pupils and encouraging them to make connections that reinforce the mathematical idea behind each core activity. The suggestions for 'making connections' with each activity will help pupils to develop a breadth of understanding and develop rich concept images for number ideas.

Reflection At the end of a session ask the pupils to explain what they have done as a way of reinforcing the activity. Remember that for some pupils with language difficulties what they can express is not always an accurate guide to *what they have understood;* there may be a discrepancy between the receptive and expressive language skills, and a pupil may have understood more than he or she is able to explain. Pupils could be encouraged to demonstrate their knowledge by manipulating Numicon Shapes or Number Rods instead of, or in addition to, explaining what they have done in words.

Practice and repetition

In order to reinforce pupils' learning it is strongly recommended that pupils have opportunities for repetition and practice several times a week, either during, or in addition to their daily small group work. Mathematical ideas are difficult because they are abstract; repetition can contribute to pupils' understanding. For pupils with significant memory difficulties, for example, it may be necessary to repeat activities twice a day (e.g., early morning and early afternoon). It should not be assumed that a pupil has understood what has been taught once; when pupils have understood it will become clear, as they will begin to enjoy practising the activities on their own.

[3] Widgit Software Ltd, www.widgit.com, accessed 30.7.08.

Self-monitoring/asking for help.

Pupils with difficulties learning mathematics should learn to self-monitor, and ask for help. As pupils move through the key stages of mainstream learning environments, the emphasis may change from being pupil-centred to becoming progressively more curriculum-centred. It is likely, in Key Stages 3 and 4, that requests for help from the pupils will become more frequent than teachers' monitoring of their learning and will become the main way of ensuring support and clarification. Learning how to ask for help and knowing when to ask for it is important, therefore. The most basic form of self-monitoring is for the pupil, in responding to a question, to say he or she does not know the answer. It is important to remind all pupils that 'I don't know' and 'I've forgotten' are legitimate responses to a question. Responding to questions can be facilitated by provision of pictorial (symbol supported) prompt cards for 'I don't know', 'I know', etc., to which a pupil can point. It is important to stress that there is no stigma in responding 'I don't know'; the ethos should be one of acknowledging that 'I don't know', or 'I've forgotten' when necessary. It is very important that the work challenges the most able pupils in the group so that they too will be forced sometimes to respond 'I don't know' (see figure 1).

Fig 1: Pupils can be given a prompt card to point to to show the teacher when they don't understand.

Assessment

'There is overwhelming evidence that arithmetical ability is not unitary: it is made up of many components, ranging from knowledge of the counting sequence, to estimation, to solving word problems. Although these components are often correlated, weaknesses can occur in any one of them. Studies have suggested that it is not possible to establish a strict hierarchy of learning in which any one component invariably precedes or follows another, *interventions that focus on the particular components with which an individual pupil has difficulty are likely to be more effective than those which assume that all pupils arithmetical difficulties are similar'* (Dowker, 2004: 15-16 – emphasis added). The Profiling Pro-forma included with the Assessment Tools included in this Kit is designed to identify the strengths and needs of individual pupils in aspects of basic mathematical understanding and also of the in-pupil factors which affect their access to mathematical teaching and learning and to help teachers record the next steps for those pupils.

The Assessment Signposts, although not designed to provide a detailed assessment do however help to indicate an appropriate starting point on the Numicon Teaching Programme. Subsequently, all pupils using the kit should have their learning continuously assessed through observation of their responses to different teaching strategies, and their attainment. This on going observation and assessment will help teachers be responsive to pupils' needs, resulting in continuous modification to the pace of teaching and the teaching strategies employed. Pupils' progress can be tracked on the Individual Record of Progress which shows the very small steps of the Teaching Programme and which is also helpful for identifying individual targets.

Many pupils with mathematical learning difficulties will learn better by 'doing' and 'seeing'. Numicon facilitates this by providing representations of number ideas that can be manipulated and visualised, enabling the pupil to move from the manual manipulation of the physical Numicon Shapes, to internal imaging and the internal manipulation of these mental images, that is, thinking about number.

6. Additional guidance on teaching approaches for specific aspects of SEN

There are particular issues that relate to specific SEN categories. Additional guidance for some of these issues is offered in this section.

In this section

Speech, language and communication needs (SLCN)

SLCN refers to the speech, language and communication needs that many pupils with SENs might have; it is not a specific category of need, like 'specific language impairment' (SLI). Most pupils described as having 'mild, moderate, severe or profound and multiple learning difficulties' (ASC or ASD), 'specific learning difficulties (dyslexia)' (SpLD), or motor organisational difficulties (dyspraxia), have speech, language and/ or communication needs, and this Numicon kit can be used to address mathematical learning needs in all these groups of pupils.

Understanding the language of mathematics underpins all mathematical learning; thus pupils who have problems with understanding and using language are likely to have significant difficulties in understanding mathematics. However, it is important to profile individual pupils because although many pupils with verbal or spatial problems may experience difficulties with mathematics, these difficulties 'cannot be used as definite predictors of either the existence or type of mathematical difficulty that a pupil may have' (Dowker, 2004: 10).

Below we provide some suggestions for teaching mathematics to pupils who have SLCN.

- Ensure that your language of instruction matches the level of the pupil's understanding.
- Use visual supports to aid the learning, retention and use of vocabulary, for example, models and images (including Numicon Shapes), signs and symbols.
- Teach concepts (e.g., more, one more than, big, bigger, biggest, small, smaller, smallest) systematically. Then teach big and not big and small and not small, but do not try initially to teach opposites together (i.e., *big* and *small*).
- Do not teach related ideas simultaneously (e.g., to teach the addition concepts *more* and *together*, first teach *more*, then teach *together*, and then explain that *add* can mean both).
- Use visual images of number size (i.e., Numicon Shapes) to support sequential learning (e.g., number lines).
- Use a visual timetable to demarcate the separate components of the day and to develop sequencing skills and language.
- When necessary, use a visual group work timetable to distinguish the various mathematical tasks in a mathematical teaching session to inhibit perseveration (getting stuck on the content of a previous task, when another has started).
- Give pupils time to respond; those with verbal comprehension and word-finding difficulties will take longer to process questions and responses.
- Make clear the sound differences between similar sounding numbers (e.g., six, sixteen, sixty) alongside using visual prompts, for example, signing and Numicon Shapes.
- Encourage self-monitoring and asking for help.

See, also, the suggestions below for teaching mathematics to pupils with motor organisational needs.

Moderate learning difficulties

A pupil with global moderate learning difficulties is likely to have speech, language and/or communication needs; therefore, all the above suggestions for pupils with SLCN apply along with the additional hints below.

- Revisit and revise areas of mathematical learning frequently; pupils with global learning difficulties often need to be 'over-taught' specific mathematical skills, concepts and knowledge.

- Take particular care of the choice of visual support to ensure that visual representations of mathematical ideas are clear and uncluttered.
- Also see the suggestions below for teaching mathematics to pupils who have motor organisational needs.

Severe and profound and multiple learning difficulties

Both the above sets of suggestions are likely to apply to pupils with severe and profound multiple learning difficulties and, although Numicon is designed for sensory motor learning, there is likely to be an even deeper focus on sensory and motor activity for these pupils. Therefore, consideration will have to be given as to how the Numicon Shapes can be explored by pupils with different levels of learning and motor needs. For example, one pupil may want to explore the size and shape of a Numicon Shape with his or her tongue; whereas another pupil may have sufficient manual motor ability to find matching pairs of Numicon Shapes in the Feely Bag. For some pupils with severe and profound difficulties it may be better that mathematics is taught as a component of personal and social life skills. In this case, consideration needs to be given to the role of Numicon within personal and social learning, for instance, when cooking relate counting spoonfuls of flour to the corresponding Numicon Shape.

Motor organisational needs (including Dyspraxia)

Organisational difficulties often underpin other areas of learning difficulty. Some pupils have specific difficulties with motor organisation and below we provide some suggestions for best practice, which could also be used when teaching any pupil who has language and/or learning difficulties.

- Place mathematical equipment (including Numicon images) on the learning surface in an organised and visually clear manner.
- Teach left to right and top to bottom organisation as the primary organisational strategy for all activities, including counting. Encourage ocular tracking by pointing with your finger (as well as visual pointing) to the start number, and pointing as you count, so that pupils can see where they need to look.
- When counting, ensure that the size and spacing of objects matches the pupils level of motor organisation.
- If necessary, start to teach counting through gross motor organisational activities, that is, counting by walking along numbered carpet tiles or Numicon Mats, and introduce concepts such as *forwards* and *backwards, one more and one less, etc.*, before practising these activities with fine motor movements, for example, using a finger to count along a table top number line.

Pupils with oral/verbal dyspraxia may be unable to pronounce words clearly – especially the words for numbers that are similar phonologically. A speech and language therapist should be consulted about how best to support individual pupils with oral/verbal dyspraxia; the appropriate strategy will depend on the stage the pupil has reached in his or her speech therapy.

ASC/ASD (including Aspergers Syndrome and Semantic-Pragmatic Disorder)

The autistic spectrum is a continuum: some pupils may have mild difficulties with social communication and understanding; social relationships, and imagination (the ASC triad of impairment); some may have profound difficulties in these areas. Pupils with autism may have comparatively few difficulties with the concrete aspects of learning or they may have learning difficulties, from mild to profound and multiple. It is very important that all the adults who may influence the pupils mathematical learning – teachers, learning support assistants, parents/carers, etc. – use the same approaches to mathematics.

Best practice for teaching mathematics to pupils with autism should use the National Autistic Society's (NAS) SPELL (Structure; Positive approaches and expectations; Empathy; Low arousal and Links) approach:[1] 'The SPELL framework can be applied across the autistic spectrum, including Aspergers syndrome. It provides a context for and is complementary to other approaches, notably TEACHC (Treatment and Education of Autistic and related Communication handicapped Children).'[2] Whilst the SPELL framework is specifically formulated for pupils with autism, many of its precepts (except, perhaps, those related to low arousal) apply to many other pupils with SEN.

Below we offer some suggestions to help in the teaching of mathematics to pupils with ASC/ASD.[3]

- Structure: use visual timetables to separate the components of a mathematics lesson to make the lesson structure clear; use visual prompts for the stages of mathematical processes, such as counting, adding, etc., which explain what needs to be done, clearly and sequentially (see figure 1).
- Be positive (in terms of approaches and expectations): identify the preferred mathematical learning style of the pupil (e.g., using sequences, looking for number patterns, using visual images for numbers, etc.). In other words, teach to the pupil's positives. Positive engagement is key to successful learning; mathematical teaching approaches should maximise pupils' levels of engagement. Build on natural strengths and interests where possible expectations should be positive, that is, high, but within a pupil's range of attainment.
- Be empathetic: try to envisage the mathematical world from the autistic pupil's point of view. What is it about mathematics that motivates or interests the pupil? What is it about number that frightens, preoccupies or distresses the pupil? If you can identify these factors mathematics can be taught in a way that the former factors are emphasised and the latter are alleviated.
- Low arousal. The mathematical approaches and the environment in which you teach, need to be calm and ordered, to reduce anxiety and support concentration. Distractions should be minimised. But 'low arousal should not be confused with no arousal' (NAS). It is important that pupils are exposed to a wide range of mathematical experiences, introduced in a planned and sensitive way. Pupils may get the greatest benefit from a teaching environment in which sensory and other stimulation can be reduced or controlled. If the colours of the Numicon Shapes interfere with the pupil's ability to focus on their size component, which is their most important feature, then photocopied Numicon Shapes should be used.
- Make links. Various aspects of the pupils' experience of mathematical learning should be linked explicitly: pupils with autism are often not able to deduce links through experiential learning, and require them to be pointed out.

Also, see the suggestions above for teaching mathematics to pupils who have SLCN.

1 For more details see: www.nas.org.uk/nas/jsp/polopoly.jsp?d=297&a=3362, accessed 2.08.2008.
2 NAS, www.nas.org.uk/nas/jsp/polopoly.jsp?d=297&a=3362, accessed 2.08.2008.
3 The structure of these points is adapted from NAS www.nas.org.uk/nas/jsp/polopoly.jsp?d=297&a=3362, accessed 2.08.2008.

Sensory needs

Not all pupils who have sensory needs will have learning difficulties and/or SLCN. For those that do, the above sets of suggestions will be useful. Here we offer some additional suggestions for pupils with sensory needs.

- Pupils with hearing needs may require extra support in the form of signing (BSL) either related to signing of the key concepts to support the spoken word, or as the main communication strategy. You should consult sensory needs specialists to agree the approach to communication and learning for a profoundly deaf pupil, to decide on the approach ('natural aural', or 'total communication' e.g., BSL). This decision will require discussion that involves the pupil and his or her parents or carers, as it will have long-term implications for the pupil's education.
- Pupils with visual needs may need printed Numicon materials to be adapted: they may need to be enlarged, or to have the text to background contrast modified. Pupils with visual needs may need more tactile experience with the Numicon Shapes. Again, the advice of the local authority's sensory needs service should be sought with regard to the individual pupil's visual needs.

Dyscalculia

The DCSF website includes the statement that:

Early indicators [of dyscalculia] will be problems dealing with sequences, problems with long-term retention of basic facts, no sense of number, an inability to see patterns in information.

Certain difficulties, for example, reading and comprehending the unique language and vocabulary of mathematics, may 'click in' after a relatively successful start in the subject. A pupil may excel at mental arithmetic and fail when required to document (or vice versa).

Different areas of mathematics may well evoke different reactions from different pupils.

It is often useful to analyse a mathematics task in terms of, for example, vocabulary, basic fact knowledge, understanding of the four operations, memory (short and long term), sequencing ability, generalising, documenting, spatial awareness, and then to identify which area creates a difficulty for the learner.

The use of Numicon in general, and this kit in particular, addresses all these indicators of dyscalculia, that is, problems with sequencing, memory, number and patterns. Use of Numicon, therefore, should assist in the teaching of mathematics to pupils diagnosed as having dyscalculia.[4]

Specific learning difficulties (Dyslexia)

The British Dyslexia Association (BDA) describes the need 'to use fingers or marks on paper to make simple calculations' after a certain age, as a possible indicator of dyslexia;[5] some pupils with dyslexia have specific difficulties with mathematics. The BDA states that, in relation to dyslexia and dyscalculia:

- Research suggests that 40-50% of dyslexics show no signs of dyscalculia. They perform at least as well in maths as other pupils, with about 10% achieving at a higher level.

---

[4] www.standards.dfes.gov.uk/primary/faqs/inclusion/56233/#56734, accessed 2.08.2008.
[5] www.bdadyslexia.org.uk/indications.html#primary, accessed 2.08.2008.

- The remaining 50-70% do have difficulties with maths. Not surprisingly, difficulty in decoding written words can transfer across into a difficulty in decoding mathematical notation and symbols.
- For some dyslexic pupils, however, difficulty with maths may in fact stem from problems with the language surrounding mathematical questions rather than with number concepts – e.g. their dyslexia may cause them to misunderstand the wording of a question.
- In summary, dyscalculia and dyslexia occur both independently of each other and together. The strategies for dealing with dyscalculia will be fundamentally the same whether or not the learner is also dyslexic.[6]

Therefore, if pupils have both dyslexia and mathematical difficulties it would seem likely that the most appropriate intervention would be to address the issues relating to mathematical notation and symbols (and the concepts that these represent), or the language of mathematics, one of the objectives of this Numicon Kit.

Specific conditions

Pupils who have specific conditions for example Down Syndrome, Fragile X Syndrome, Cerebral Palsy, etc. may well present with aspects of one or more of the special needs described throughout this section.

Numicon is recommended by the Down Syndrome Educational Trust because the strong patterns of the Numicon Shapes appeal to visual memory, which is often a relative strength in pupils who have this syndrome. Numicon is likely also to be useful for other groups of pupils who have conditions that result in their having relative strengths in visual memory.

6 www.bdadyslexia.org.uk/dyscalculia.html, accessed on 2.08.2008.

7. Not a conclusion!

Because this teaching guide does not follow a narrative thread, there is not a natural conclusion. It is hoped that having read it through, teachers will continue to dip in and out of the material, picking out advice appropriate to their various pupils. We hope that the advice is helpful and that teachers using Closing the Gap with Numicon and our other Numicon kits will enjoy teaching the activities and also find that their pupils make good progress. We would be delighted to hear how you get on and welcome your ideas and suggestions. You can communicate with us via the Numicon website www.numicon.com where there is a users' forum for sharing ideas and discussion.

Appendix A: Key mathematical vocabulary with suggested signs and symbols

Key mathematical vocabulary	Sign systems (and adaptation where applicable)	Symbol systems
Number 0-10	Makaton [1]	Standard English numerals **and** Numicon Shapes
Number 11 and 12 (standard spoken English)	British Sign Language [2]	
Numbers 13-19 (standard spoken English)	British Sign Language (adapted: Makaton-style hand shapes for 13-19 'flap', at 90 degrees to normal, in British Sign Language style movement for 13-19)	
Numbers 11 to 19 (intermediate step to counting competence: …eight, nine, ten, ten one, ten two, ten three, ten four… etc.)	Makaton (Adapted: Signed with the ten first)	
Numbers 20 onwards (standard spoken English)	Makaton	
Big/Small	Makaton	Widget/Rebus [3]
Bigger/Smaller	Makaton (adapted: Replace finger spelling of 'er' with a small additional 'jump' of the hands in the direction of hand travel (outwards for bigger; inwards for smaller)	Widget/Rebus
Biggest/Smallest	Makaton (adapted: Replace finger spelling of 'er' with a small additional 'jump' of the hands in the direction of hand travel (outwards for bigger; inwards for smaller)	Widget/Rebus
More/Less	Makaton	Makaton [4] (Standard mathematical symbols)
Odd/Even	Makaton	Makaton
Add/Subtract	Numicon signs	Standard mathematical symbols
Equals/is equivalent to (is of equal value)	Numicon sign	Standard mathematical symbols
Same ('same' does not mean equal)	Makaton sign	Rebus

Bibliography

Atkinson, R., Tacon, R., Wing, A. (2004) 'Learning about numbers with patterns' – summary of original classroom based research project which led to the development of the Numicon Teaching Programme. BEAM Research Paper RES04, BEAM Education, available at www.numicon.com/abouthtenumiconapproach/research.html, accessed 7.06.2008.

Bone, C., Chapman, C. and Saunders, S. (2006) Visual Images and Models Supported by Signs and Symbols. Brighton: Brighton and Hove City Council.

Bristow, J., Cowley, P. and Daines, B. (1999) Memory and Learning: A practical guide for teachers. London: David Fulton.

British Dyslexia Association (BDA), Indications of Dyslexia www.bdadyslexia.org.uk/indications.html#primary, accessed 2.08.2008.

British Dyslexia Association (BDA), Dyscalculia, Dyslexia and Maths www.bdadyslexia.org.uk/dyscalculia.html, accessed 2.08.2008.

Butterworth, B. (2005) 'The development of arithmetic abilities', Journal of Pupil Psychology and Psychiatry 46(1): 3-18.

Cumbria County Council, Development of Attention Control, www.cumbria.gov.uk/elibrary/Content/Internet/537/705/1109/1111/1114/37965143848.pdf, accessed 8.08.2008.

Qualifications and Curriculum Authority (QCA) National Curriculum Inclusion Statement, curriculum.qca.org.uk/key-stages-1-and-2/inclusion/statutory-inclusion-statement, accessed 5.08.2008.

Department for Children, Schools and Families, Primary National Strategy, Primary Framework for Literacy and Mathematics, at www.standards.dfes.gov.uk/primaryframeworks/mathematics/, accessed 2.08.2008.

Department for Children, Schools and Families, Primary National Strategy, Mathematics, Dyslexia and Dyscalculia, at www.standards.dfes.gov.uk/primary/faqs/inclusion/56233/#56734, accessed 2.08.2008.

Dowker, A. (2004) What Works for Pupils with Mathematical Difficulties? Department for Education and Skills, Research Report 554. London: Department for Education and Skills.

Grauberg, E. (1998) Elementary Mathematics and Language Difficulties: A book for teachers, therapists and parents. London: Whurr Publishers Ltd.

Haring, N.G., Lovitt, T.C., Eaton, M.D. and Hansen, C.L. (1978) The Fourth R: Research in the classroom. Columbus, OH: Charles E. Merrill Publishing Co.

Makaton (1993a) National Curriculum Book of Signs. Camberley: Makaton Vocabulary Development Project.

Makaton (1993b) National Curriculum Book of Symbols. Camberley: Makaton Vocabulary Development Project.

Makaton (2008) Makaton for Maths Guidelines, Camberley: Makaton Vocabulary Development Project.

National Autistic Society (NAS), SPELL, at www.nas.org.uk/nas/jsp/polopoly.jsp?d=297&a=3362, accessed 2.08.2008.

Piaget, J. (1952) The Child's Conception of Number. London: Routledge and Kegan Paul.

Rinaldi, W. (2005) Language Concepts to Access Learning. Cranleigh, available from the author (18 Dorking Road, Chilwroth, Surrey, CU4 8NR).

Rinaldi, W. (2005) Social Use of Language Programme: Infant and Primary School (SULP-IP). Cranleigh: available from the author (18 Dorking Road, Chilwroth, Surrey, CU4 8NR).

Smith, C., and Hodgson, D. (1998) Communication Link: Dictionary of signs Beverley: Beverley School.

Widget Software, Writing with Symbols 2000, at www.widgit.com/products/wws2000/index.htm, accessed 2.08.2008.

Acknowledgements

We acknowledge the contribution of Clare Chapman, Educational Psychologist, Brighton and Hove City Council for invaluable help and advice.

Key to the Activities

Title

The Title indicates the broad scope of the activities on the card.

Key mathematical ideas

Refer to Section 2 of the Teaching Guide for explanation of the key mathematical ideas pupils are meeting through each activity and the aspects of the ideas that pupils are likely to find challenging.

Aim

The intended learning pupils should achieve.

The activities

The core activities are described step by step. Many activities will need to be repeated and practised many times before the aim is achieved.

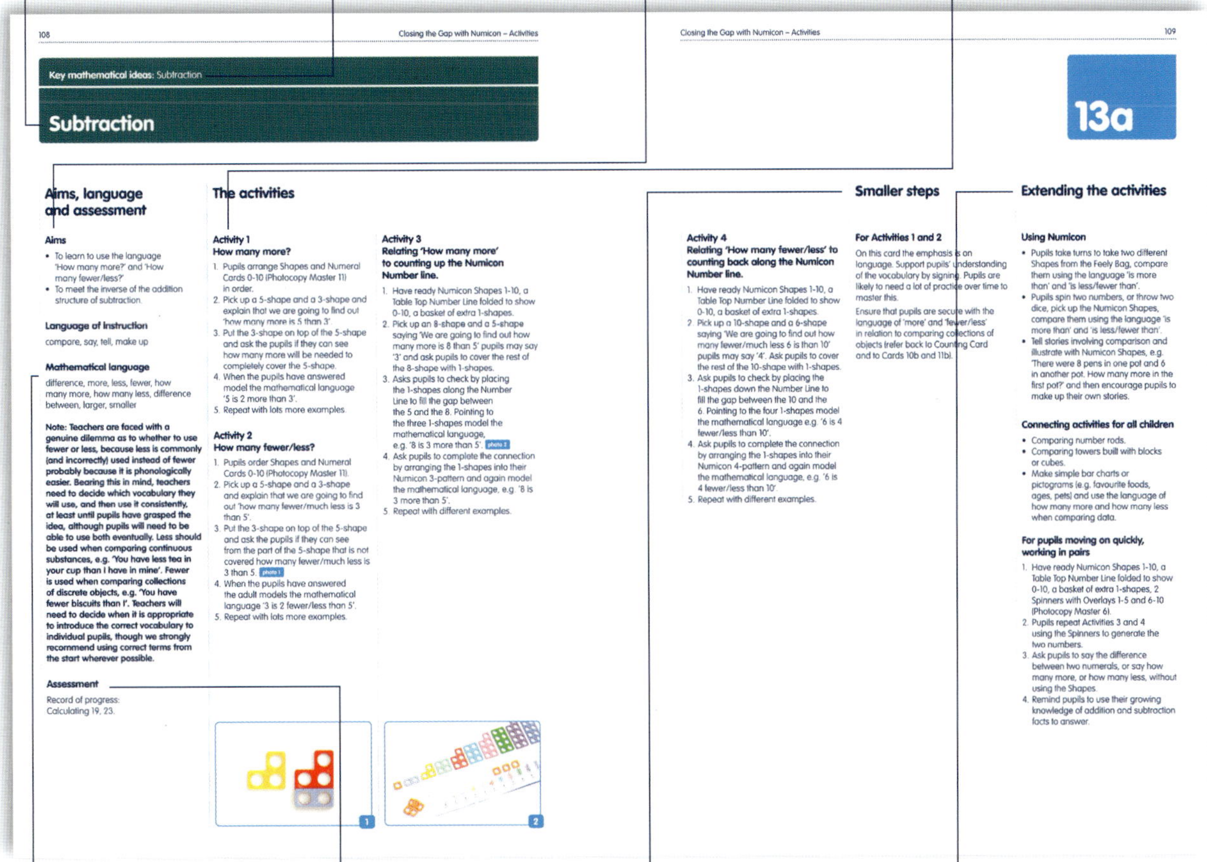

108 Closing the Gap with Numicon – Activities

Key mathematical ideas: Subtraction

Subtraction

Aims, language and assessment

Aims

- To learn to use the language 'How many more?' and 'How many fewer/less?'
- To meet the inverse of the addition structure of subtraction.

Language of instruction

compare, say, tell, make up

Mathematical language

difference, more, less, fewer, how many more, how many less, difference between, larger, smaller

Note: Teachers are faced with a genuine dilemma as to whether to use fewer or less, because less is commonly (and incorrectly) used instead of fewer probably because it is phonologically easier. Bearing this in mind, teachers need to decide which vocabulary they will use, and then use it consistently, at least until pupils have grasped the idea, although pupils will need to be able to use both eventually. Less should be used when comparing continuous substances, e.g. 'You have less tea in your cup than I have in mine'. Fewer is used when comparing collections of discrete objects, e.g. 'You have fewer biscuits than I'. Teachers will need to decide when it is appropriate to introduce the correct vocabulary to individual pupils, though we strongly recommend using correct terms from the start wherever possible.

Assessment

Record of progress: Calculating 19, 23.

The activities

Activity 1
How many more?

1. Pupils arrange Shapes and Numeral Cards 0-10 (Photocopy Master 11) in order.
2. Pick up a 5-shape and a 3-shape and explain that we are going to find out 'how many more is 5 than 3'.
3. Put the 3-shape on top of the 5-shape and ask the pupils if they can see how many more will be needed to completely cover the 5-shape.
4. When the pupils have answered model the mathematical language '5 is 2 more than 3'.
5. Repeat with lots more examples.

Activity 2
How many fewer/less?

1. Pupils order Shapes and Numeral Cards 0-10 (Photocopy Master 11).
2. Pick up a 5-shape and a 3-shape and explain that we are going to find out 'how many fewer/much less is 3 than 5'.
3. Put the 3-shape on top of the 5-shape and ask the pupils if they can see from the part of the 5-shape that is not covered how many fewer/much less is 3 than 5. photo 1
4. When the pupils have answered the adult models the mathematical language '3 is 2 fewer/less than 5'.
5. Repeat with lots more examples.

Activity 3
Relating 'How many more' to counting up the Numicon Number line.

1. Have ready Numicon Shapes 1-10, a Table Top Number Line folded to show 0-10, a basket of extra 1-shapes.
2. Pick up an 8-shape and a 5-shape saying 'We are going to find out how many more is 8 than 5' pupils may say '3' and ask pupils to cover the rest of the 8-shape with 1-shapes.
3. Asks pupils to check by placing the 1-shapes along the Number Line to fill the gap between the 5 and the 8. Pointing to the three 1-shapes model the mathematical language, e.g. '8 is 3 more than 5'. photo 2
4. Ask pupils to complete the connection by arranging the 1-shapes into their Numicon 3-pattern and again model the mathematical language, e.g. '8 is 3 more than 5'.
5. Repeat with different examples.

1

2

Closing the Gap with Numicon – Activities 109

13a

Activity 4
Relating 'How many fewer/less' to counting back along the Numicon Number line.

1. Have ready Numicon Shapes 1-10, a Table Top Number Line folded to show 0-10, a basket of extra 1-shapes.
2. Pick up a 10-shape and a 6-shape saying 'We are going to find out how many fewer/much less 6 is than 10' pupils may say '4'. Ask pupils to cover the rest of the 10-shape with 1-shapes.
3. Ask pupils to check by placing the 1-shapes down the Number Line to fill the gap between the 10 and the 6. Pointing to the four 1-shapes model the mathematical language e.g. '6 is 4 fewer/less than 10'.
4. Ask pupils to complete the connection by arranging the 1-shapes into their Numicon 4-pattern and again model the mathematical language, e.g. '6 is 4 fewer/less than 10'.
5. Repeat with different examples.

Smaller steps

For Activities 1 and 2

On this card the emphasis is on language. Support pupils' understanding of the vocabulary by signing. Pupils are likely to need a lot of practice over time to master this.

Ensure that pupils are secure with the language of 'more' and 'fewer/less' in relation to comparing collections of objects (refer back to Counting Card and to Cards 10b and 11b).

Extending the activities

Using Numicon

- Pupils take turns to take two different Shapes from the Feely Bag, compare them using the language 'is more than' and 'is less/fewer than'.
- Pupils spin two numbers, or throw two dice, pick up the Numicon Shapes, compare them using the language 'is more than' and 'is less/fewer than'.
- Tell stories involving comparison and illustrate with Numicon Shapes, e.g. 'There were 8 pens in one pot and 6 in another pot. How many more in the first pot?' and then encourage pupils to make up their own stories.

Connecting activities for all children

- Comparing number rods.
- Comparing towers built with blocks or cubes.
- Make simple bar charts or pictograms (e.g. favourite foods, ages, pets) and use the language of how many more and how many less when comparing data.

For pupils moving on quickly, working in pairs

1. Have ready Numicon Shapes 1-10, a Table Top Number Line folded to show 0-10, a basket of extra 1-shapes, 2 Spinners with Overlays 1-5 and 6-10 (Photocopy Master 6).
2. Pupils repeat Activities 3 and 4 using the Spinners to generate the two numbers.
3. Ask pupils to say the difference between two numerals, or say how many more, or how many less, without using the Shapes.
4. Remind pupils to use their growing knowledge of addition and subtraction facts to answer.

Language

Both the language of instruction and the mathematical language are shown on each activity. The language of instruction is used to explain to pupils what they have to do. The language of mathematics expresses the mathematics that pupils are learning.

Assessment

A cross-reference to the Numicon Record of Progress in the Assessment Tools section of the Kit.

Smaller steps

Some pupils who have special needs benefit from following these smaller steps. Pre-teaching ideas are suggested for some activities.

Extending the activities

Connecting activities and Using Numicon are suitable for the majority of pupils. And the challenge can be increased further for pupils moving on quickly.

Activity Summary

The Closing the Gap with Numicon Activities are Summarised below. The first four Activities on Counting and Pattern are ongoing and run concurrently with the rest of the programme. The remaining Activities can be followed in order.

Counting A

Activity title
Counting

Key mathematical ideas
Counting

Aims
To learn to recite the number names in order (the count sequence).

To begin to learn to count one to one.

Counting B

Activity title
Counting

Key mathematical ideas
Counting, Cardinal property of number

Aims

To learn to count one to one.

To begin to use 'more' and 'fewer' or 'less' when comparing number values.

To understand that the last number of the count tells you its size (cardinal value).

Pattern A

Activity title
Pattern

Key mathematical ideas
Pattern

Aim
To learn to copy, continue and devise repeating patterns.

Pattern B

Activity title
Pattern and Sequence

Key mathematical ideas
Pattern

Aims
To develop visual spatial perception and organisational skills.

To develop understanding of direction.

1a

Activity title
Getting to Know the Numicon Shapes

Key mathematical ideas
Pattern, Shape

Aims
To explore freely the Numicon Shapes.

1b

Activity title
Getting to Know the Numicon Shapes

Key mathematical ideas
Pattern, Order, Shape

Aims
To learn to match Numicon Shapes by colour and shape.

2a

Activity title
Getting to Know the Numicon Shapes

Key mathematical ideas
Pattern, Order, Space

Aims
To match Numicon Shapes to coloured pictures of the Shapes.

2b

Activity title
Getting to Know the Numicon Shapes

Key mathematical ideas
Order, Comparison

Aims
To understand and use the language 'bigger' with Numicon.

3a

Activity title
Getting to Know the Numicon Shapes

Key mathematical ideas
Order, Comparison

Aims
To understand and use the language 'smaller' with Numicon.

3b

Activity title
Getting to Know the Numicon Shapes

Key mathematical ideas
Order, Comparison

Aims
To use the language of comparative size with Numicon.

4a

Activity title
Learning to Order the Numicon Shapes

Key mathematical ideas
Order, Comparison

Aims
To put Numicon Shapes in order of size.

4b

Activity title
Learning to Order the Numicon Shapes

Key mathematical ideas
Order, Comparison

Aims
To order Numicon Shapes confidently and securely.

5a

Activity title
Getting to Know the Numicon Shapes and Patterns

Key mathematical ideas
Pattern, Shape

Aims
To match Numicon Shapes to grey pictures of the Shapes, outlines of the Shapes, and small representations of the Numicon patterns as shown on the Spinner Overlays.

5b

Activity title
Getting to Know the Numicon Shapes and Patterns

Key mathematical ideas
Pattern, Shape

Aim
To learn the patterns of the Numicon Shapes.

6a

Activity title
Giving the Numicon Shapes their Number Names

Key mathematical ideas
Counting

Aim
To give number names to the Numicon Shapes and to count objects one by one.

6b

Activity title
Knowing the Number Names of the Numicon Shapes

Key mathematical ideas
Order, Addition, Equivalence

Aims
To call the Numicon Shapes by their number names with confidence and when using them in a variety of situations.

7a

Activity title
Ordering the Numicon Shapes and Numerals

Key mathematical ideas
Order

Aims
To match numerals with Numicon Shapes in order.

7b

Activity title
Knowing the Numicon Patterns and Numerals

Key mathematical ideas
Moving beyond counting

Aims
To practise connecting Numicon Shapes, number names and numerals without counting.

8a

Activity title
Knowing the Numicon Patterns and Numerals

Key mathematical ideas
Pattern, Moving beyond counting

Aims
To be confident about recognising Numicon Shapes and patterns, using number names and recognising numerals.

8b

Activity title
Using the Numicon Patterns

Key mathematical ideas
Pattern, Moving beyond counting

Aims
To prepare pupils for place value.

To see that arranging objects into patterns or grouping is an efficient way to find out 'how many'.

9a

Activity title
Using the Numicon Patterns

Key mathematical ideas
Pattern, Moving beyond counting

Aims
To use their mental imagery of the Numicon patterns.

To develop mathematical reasoning.

To begin to use the language for addition and subtraction.

9b

Activity title
Addition

Key mathematical ideas
Addition

Aims
To relate addition to combining two or more Shapes and to use the language of addition.

To know that addition is used to answer 'How many altogether?'

10a

Activity title
Addition

Key mathematical ideas
Addition

Aims
To relate addition to combining two or more Shapes and to use the language of addition.

To use mathematical reasoning.

10b

Activity title
Addition

Key mathematical ideas
Addition

Aims
To find 1 more than a number from 1-9.

To introduce the increase structure of addition.

11a

Activity title
Addition

Key mathematical ideas
Addition, Pattern

Aims
To see doubles as special combinations of two numbers.

11b

Activity title
Subtraction

Key mathematical ideas
Subtraction as Taking Away

Aims
To relate subtraction to taking away, using the vocabulary involved in subtraction.

To know that subtraction is used to answer 'How many left?'

12a

Activity title
Subtraction

Key mathematical ideas
Subtraction

Aims
To find 1 fewer/less than any number from 1-10.

To meet the decrease structure of subtraction.

12b

Activity title
Subtraction

Key mathematical ideas
Subtraction as difference

Aims
To begin to understand the comparison and difference structure of subtraction.

13a

Activity title Subtraction

Key mathematical ideas Subtraction

Aims
To learn to use the language 'How many more?' and 'How many fewer/less?'

To meet the inverse of addition structure of subtraction.

13b

Activity title
Reasoning About Numbers

Key mathematical ideas
Comparison, Number, Mathematical thinking

Aims
To begin to reason logically about numbers

To understand bigger and smaller in the context of numbers.

Key mathematical ideas: Counting

Counting

Aims, language and assessment

Aims

- To learn to recite the number names in order (the count sequence).
- To begin to learn to count one to one.

Language of instruction

count, say

Mathematical language

count, number names, how many, more, enough, not enough, match, find, next, before, after

Assessment

Record of Progress:
Numbers and The Number System
1, 6, 26, 33.

The activities

Note: Counting should form part of pupils' daily number experiences, so activities on this and the following card continue in parallel with other Closing the Gap activities. Support pupils' counting and numeral recognition by creating a number rich environment.

- Remember to find the last number in counts on the Numicon Number Line.
- Use numerals to label how many pupils may work on certain activities, e.g. the computer.
- Number drawers as well as naming them.
- Number storage pots for pencils, crayons, scissors, etc. to show how many.
- Make sure there are plenty of objects around which use number in everyday situations, e.g. calendars, clocks, timetables, the register, and refer to them frequently.
- Display different number lines and number friezes, e.g. Numicon Number Lines, 0-100 number line, 1-100 number square, and draw pupils' attention to them frequently.
- Refer to the Teaching Guide, page 32, for ideas on creating appropriate learning environments.
- Use the environment by asking questions such as: How many pupils are here today? How many books shall we read today? How many pieces of fruit do we have?

Learning to recite the count sequence

- Sing counting songs and learn counting rhymes.
- Look at counting books, read counting stories.

Numeral recognition

As well as displaying the Numicon Number Line, set up a counting display to help pupils connect each numeral with its Numicon Shape and pattern. Number dominoes, Number lotto, Number puzzles.

To help pupils recognise numerals and begin to say one number word for each object counted (count one to one), make a little counting book for each number, initially from 1-5 extending to 10.

Counting objects one to one

- Introduce one to one matching through everyday opportunities such as matching one straw to each drink, one biscuit to each plate, etc.
- Use Photocopy Master 1 for pupils to match one object to each circle (vary by using different objects e.g. buttons, play people, balls of playdough, etc.) photo 1
- Walk the Numicon Number Line. Place Numicon Shapes 1-10 in order on the floor. Ask pupils to count as they step from Shape to Shape. To vary: colour, cut out and laminate Numicon Shapes (Photocopy Master 2) to make mats.
- Use the Table Top Number Line folded to show only 0-5, ask pupils to place one object on each number. Extend to 10 as pupils are ready.
- Counting stairs and steps. Prepare mats showing the numerals and matching Numicon Shapes. Put on the wall by the appropriate stair so pupils can learn to count as they go upstairs.
- Mark containers to show how many they should contain so when pupils are tidying up they can count to check that the right numbers of pencils, paintbrushes, scissors, etc. are in each.

Counting A

- Give pupils seven or eight counters to count in any order. Ask them to start at different points in the row of objects, and finish at different points.
- Provide different objects for pupils to count; they can take a handful, fill a pot, take a basket of objects, and then count to find out how many. It is helpful for pupils to place objects along a number line or number track as they count (Photocopy Masters 3 and 4). photo 2
- Playing board games.
- Extend counting to 20 if pupils are able.

Counting on (and back from)...

When pupils are secure in reciting the count sequence 1-10 they need to learn to count on from any number within this range. Put a set of Numicon Shapes 1-10 in order, point to one of the Shapes for the pupil to count on from. When pupils are confident to do this with the Numicon Shapes move on to doing the same activity with the Numicon Large Format Table Top Number Line, and then with the Number Track (Photocopy Master 4). Eventually repeat the activities counting backwards from a number.

1

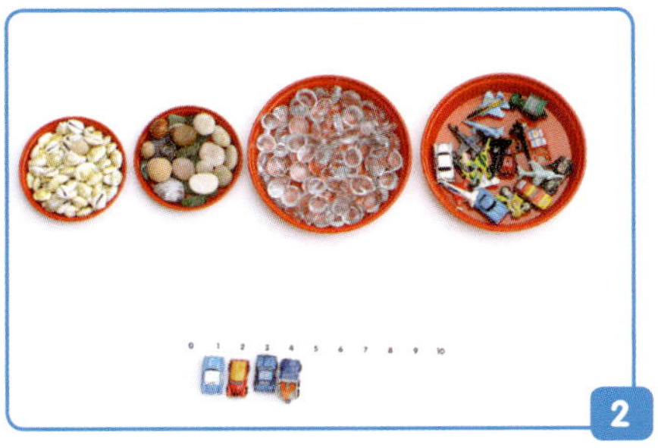

2

Smaller steps

- If pupils have difficulty remembering the count sequence from 1–10, it is helpful for teachers to model saying it quickly so pupils can hold the full sequence in their short term memory.
- For pupils who have phonological memory difficulties who find it difficult to remember the count sequence, introducing numerals and Numicon Shapes as well as the number names provides them with two visual prompts on which to hang the sounds of the number words.

Extending the activities

For pupils moving on quickly

Follow Numicon Kit 1, Numbers and The Number System Cards 1A and 1B. In order to encourage pupils to extend their counting range support their counting with number lines and give them larger collections of objects to count, until they are confident in counting clearly one to one, to at least 30.

Key mathematical ideas: Counting, Cardinal property of number

Counting

Aims, language and assessment

Aims

- To learn to count one to one.
- To begin to use 'more' and 'fewer' or 'less' when comparing number values.
- To understand that the last number of the count tells you its size (cardinal value).

Language of instruction

compare, say, tell, make up

Mathematical language

count, number names, how many, more, less, fewer, enough, not enough, match, find, next, before, after, too many, too few, most, least

Note: Teachers are faced with a genuine dilemma as to whether to use fewer or less, because less is commonly (and incorrectly) used instead of fewer probably because it is phonologically easier. Bearing this in mind, teachers need to decide which vocabulary they will use, and then use it consistently, at least until pupils have grasped the idea, although pupils will need to be able to use both eventually. Less should be used when comparing continuous substances, e.g. 'You have less tea in your cup than I have in mine'. Fewer is used when comparing collections of discrete objects, e.g. 'You have fewer biscuits than I'. Teachers will need to decide when it is appropriate to introduce the correct vocabulary to individual pupils, though we strongly recommend using correct terms from the start wherever possible.

Assessment

Record of Progress:
Numbers and The Number System 1, 6, 8, 19, 21, 28, 36.

The activities

Activity 1
More holes, fewer/less holes

1. Have ready two different sized Shapes. Count the holes in each and ask pupils which is bigger and which is smaller. Explain that the bigger Shape has more holes and the smaller Shape has fewer/less holes.
2. Repeat with other Shapes asking pupils which has more holes and which has fewer/less holes.

Activity 2
How many ones?

1. Have ready a basket of ten 1-shapes, a Baseboard and a set of Numicon Shapes 1-10
2. Pupils take a handful of 1-shapes and find out how many by counting them as they place them along the Number Line.
3. Pupils then move the 1-shapes and arrange them into the Numicon pattern on the Baseboard. Check by finding the equivalent Numicon Shape and placing it on top of the 1-shapes. Discuss with pupils who has 'more' 1-shapes and who has 'fewer/less'. photo 1
4. When pupils are confident arranging the 1-shapes into the Numicon patterns on the Baseboard, they can arrange them on the table top.
5. Find the number on Numicon Number Line.

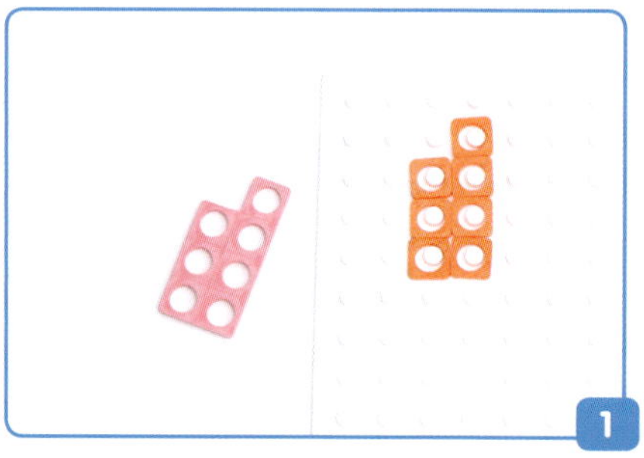
1

Activity 3
Who has more? Who has fewer/less?

1. Have ready a Table Top Number Line for every pupil, and 4 baskets each containing Pegs of one colour.
2. Each pupil chooses a colour and takes a handful of Pegs. Pupils find out how many they have by placing their Pegs along their Number Lines.
3. Pupils compare to see who has more Pegs and who has fewer. When more than two pupils are playing the words 'most' and 'least' can be introduced.
4. Pupils arrange their Pegs into the Numicon pattern, check with the Numicon Shape, and find the number on the Display Number Line.

Counting
B

Smaller steps

Activity 1

- Before embarking on this activity check that pupils understand 'more' in terms of quantity. Have ready a basket of Pegs, give each pupil a handful, then ask them to take some 'more'. Repeat, asking them to pick up one more.
- The relative language of 'more' and 'fewer/less' is difficult for some pupils to understand. Some pupils may need first to concentrate only on identifying who has 'more' and then repeat the activity concentrating on identifying who has 'fewer/less'.
- Make two collections of objects, one with many (ten or more) and one with very few (two or three). Discuss and compare the size of the collections and ask pupils which collection has more and which has fewer/less, encouraging them to use the language.
- If pupils have fine motor difficulties, give them two enlarged card Shapes (enlarge Shapes using Photocopy Master 2), and ask pupils to count balls of plasticine on to the 'holes'; compare the two filled Shapes and say which has more and which has less/fewer.

Extending the activities

For pupils moving on quickly

Ask pupils to count collections of objects without the support of the number line.

Repeat the activities on Counting A and extend to include 'teen' numbers. When pupils are secure in the count sequence to 20 follow Numicon Kit 1, Numbers and The Number System Cards 1A-3B.

Key mathematical ideas: Pattern

Pattern and Sequence

Aims, language and assessment

Aims

To learn to copy, continue and devise repeating patterns.

Language of instruction

copy, match, arrange, continue

Mathematical language

the same, pattern, too many, too few, enough, not enough, next, before, after

Assessment

Record of Progress:
Using Pattern 12, 13, 14, 15, 16, 17, 18, 19, 20.

The activities

Note: Ability to create and recognise patterns and sequences is key to understanding number, therefore the activities on this and the next card continue in parallel with all other Closing the Gap activities.

Activity 1
Copying a simple repeating pattern

1. Have ready a Baseboard and baskets of Pegs sorted by colour.
2. Make a repeating pattern on the Baseboard for pupils to copy. Discuss the pattern with the pupils pointing to and saying the pattern aloud – red, yellow, red, yellow, etc. photo 1

Activity 2
Continuing a simple repeating pattern

1. Have ready a Baseboard and baskets of Pegs sorted by colour.
2. Start a simple repeating pattern and ask pupils what colour the next Peg will be. Pupils continue the pattern. Encourage the correct use of language.

Activity 3
Devising a simple repeating pattern

1. Have ready a Baseboard and baskets of Pegs sorted by colour.
2. Pupils devise their own repeating patterns.

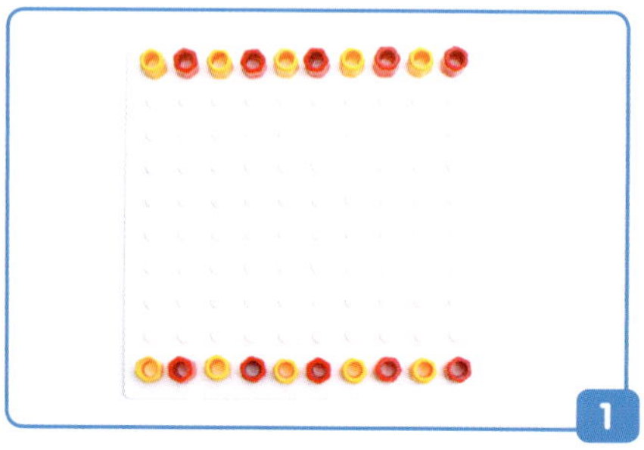

1

Pattern
A

Smaller steps

If pupils have fine motor difficulties these activities could be followed replacing the Baseboard with a square grid drawn on card (or enlarged from Photocopy Master 9 or 10) and replacing the Pegs with balls of plasticine or other suitable objects. photo 2

Extending the activities

Connecting activities for all children

- Use different materials to devise repeating patterns e.g. threading beads, printing, pegboards.
- Develop patterns and sequences in movement and with percussion instruments.
- Sound stories.
- Singing songs with repeated sequences.

For pupils moving on quickly

- Pupils build patterns with more than two colours of Pegs, and with different numbers of Pegs. photo 3
- Prepare collections of natural objects for pupils to use in creating repeating patterns. photo 4
- Continue with the work on repeating patterns in Numicon Kit 1, Using Pattern Cards 1a-2b.

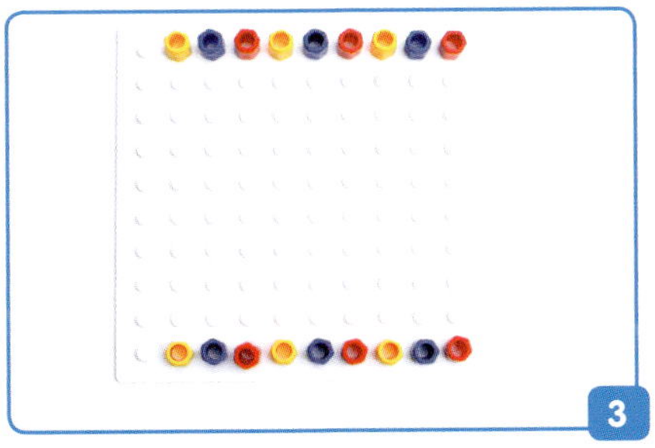
3

2

4

Key mathematical ideas: Pattern

Pattern and Sequence

Aims, language and assessment

Aims

- To develop visual spatial perception and organisational skills.
- To develop understanding of direction.

Language of instruction

copy, match, arrange

Mathematical language

the same, pattern, too many, too few, enough, not enough, next, before, after, direction, diagonal, across, corner, edge, down

Assessment

Record of Progress:
Using Pattern 12, 13, 14, 15, 16, 17, 18, 19, 20, 21, 24, 25, 26, 27.

The activities

Note: Over several lessons give pupils opportunities to copy the arrangements of Pegs in the ways illustrated below.

Have ready two Baseboards and baskets of Pegs sorted by colour and make different arrangements for pupils to copy. photos 1-7

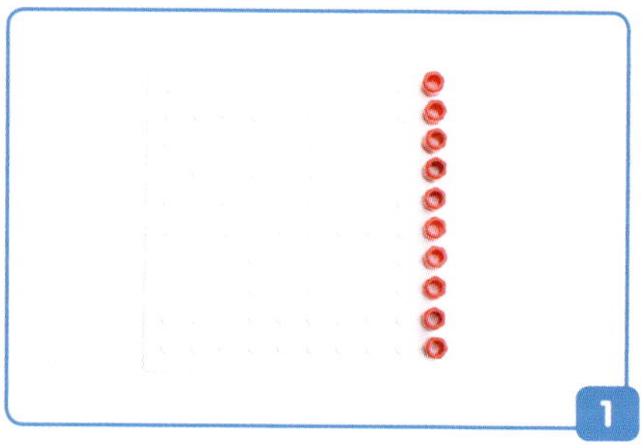
1

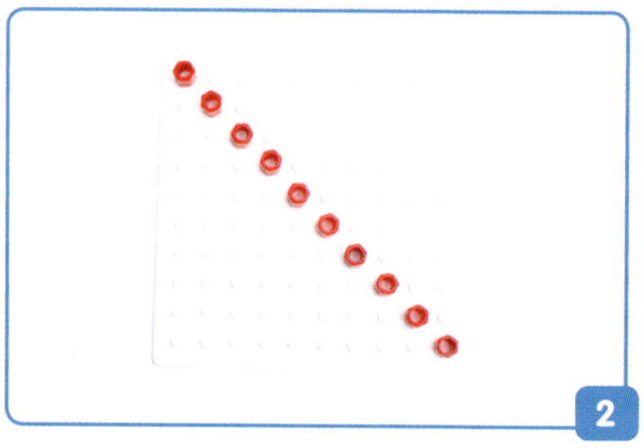
2

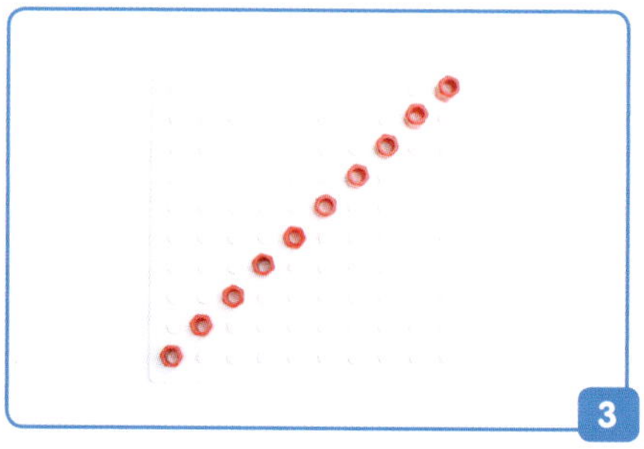
3

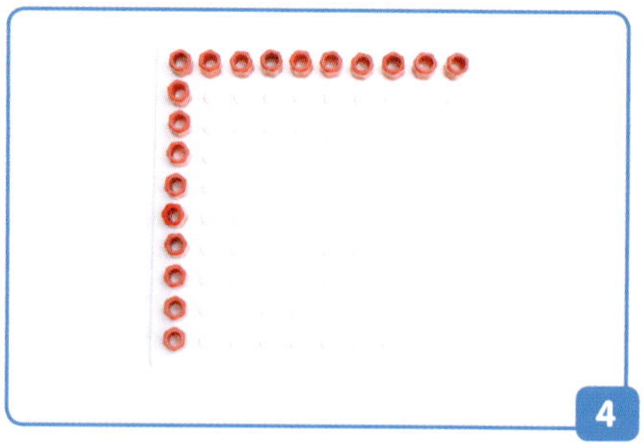
4

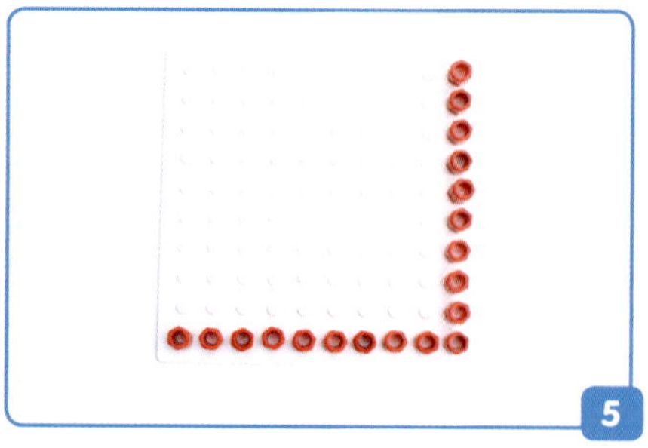
5

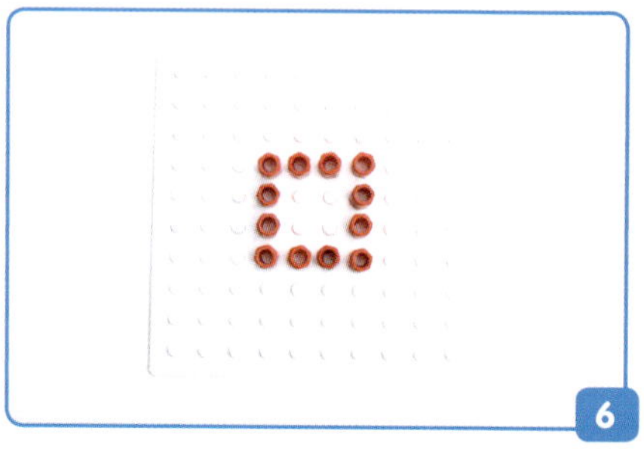
6

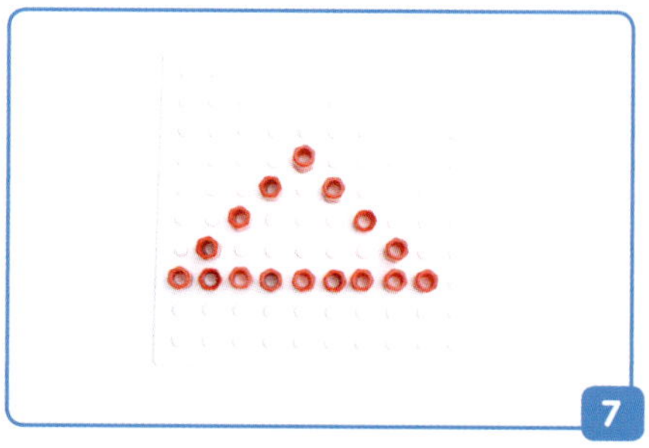
7

Pattern
B

Smaller steps

If pupils have fine motor difficulties these activities could be followed by replacing the Baseboard with a square grid drawn on card (or enlarged Photocopy Master 9 or 10) and replacing the Pegs with balls of plasticine or other suitable objects.

Extending the activities

Connecting activities for all children

- In PE play games where pupils have to respond to directional language, e.g. running diagonally across the hall; rolling a hoop or ball in different directions.
- Use a variety of media (drawing, painting, plasticine, craft materials such as matchsticks, string, lolly sticks) for pupils to create patterns where lines go in different directions, e.g. zigzags, straight line patterns, wavy line patterns, use matchsticks to create triangle patterns, straight line patterns, e.g. alternating horizontal, vertical, horizontal, vertical.

For pupils moving on quickly

- Invite pupils to make their own arrangements with Pegs on the Baseboard.
- Repeat the seven arrangements shown opposite using repeating patterns instead of single colours. photo 8
- Give pupils five, six, seven, eight, nine or ten counters to make different arrangements on a table top – these could be recorded. Continue with the work on repeating patterns in Numicon Kit 1, Using Pattern Cards 1a-2b.

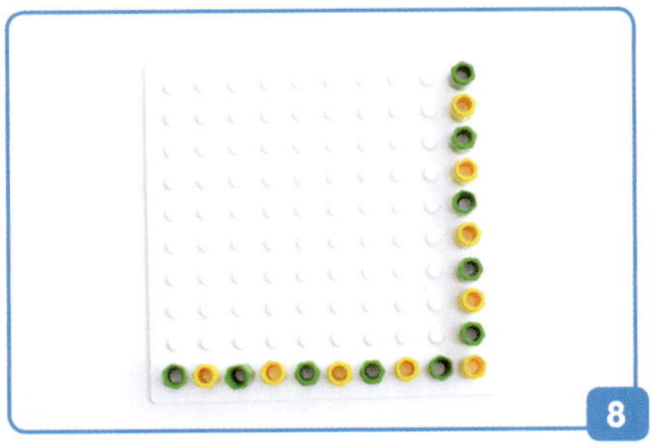
8

Key mathematical ideas: Pattern, Shape

Getting to Know the Numicon Shapes

Aims, language and assessment

Aims

To explore freely the Numicon Shapes.

Language of instruction

on, in, turn over, turn round

Mathematical language

big, small, the same size, the same shape

Assessment

This activity is not related specifically to the Assessment Signposts as it is for early familiarisation, though there are opportunities for developing language of size and comparison.

Record of Progress:
Using Pattern 1, 2, 3.

The activities

Note: If pupils use number names as they handle the Shapes, acknowledge the correct use of these number names. Rectify incorrect use of number names by modelling back the correct name to avoid repeated rehearsal of incorrect vocabulary.

Activity 1
Cover the board

Put out a Baseboard and a basket of mixed Shapes (include more 1 and 2 Shapes) for pupils to fill the board with Numicon Shapes. photo 1

Smaller steps

- Use only part of the board, covering some of it with card or by making a border with 10-shapes. photo 2
- Use only 1-shapes and 2-shapes; gradually increase to include more.
- If rotating the 'odd' shapes is too challenging, first use 'even' Shapes and introduce the 'odd' Shapes gradually, including plenty of 1-shapes.
- When pupils are working with all the number Shapes ensure that there are more of the 1 and 2-shapes.

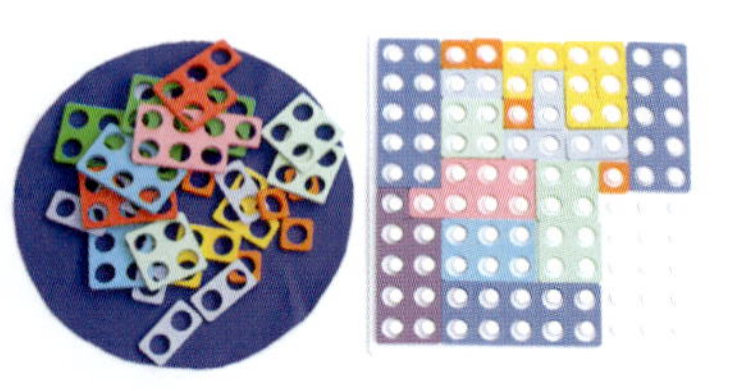
1

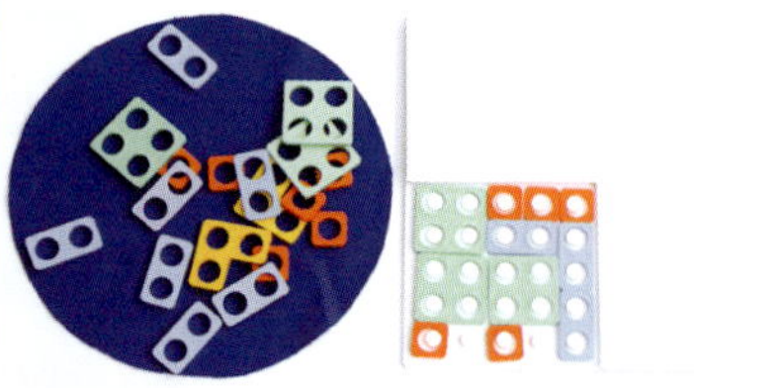
2

1a

Extending the activities

Using Numicon

- Put Numicon Shapes on a magnetic board for pupils to rearrange.
- Display the Numicon Display Number Line so pupils begin to notice the Numicon Shapes.
- Encourage pupils to create their own pictures and patterns with Numicon Shapes, both on and off the Baseboard.

Connecting activities for all children

- Puzzles where pupils have to look carefully at and rotate shapes, e.g. one-piece inset puzzles, multi-piece inset puzzles where two or more pieces are fitted into a shape, geometric-shape, puzzles e.g. shape posting boxes,
- Tangrams (if appropriate make simple 2 or 3 piece tangrams from card).

For pupils moving on quickly

- Limit the number of 1 and 2-Shapes.
- Limit the variety of Shapes used, e.g. omit 6 and 7 Shapes. Vary by omitting different sets of Shapes.
- Give pupils only two of each Shape.
- Encourage pupils to begin to identify Numicon Shapes by touch. Pupils take Shapes, one by one, from the Feely Bag to cover the Baseboard.

Key mathematical ideas: Pattern, Order, Shape

Getting to Know the Numicon Shapes

Aims, language and assessment

Aims

To learn to match Numicon Shapes by colour and shape.

Language of instruction

on top, underneath, feel, match

Mathematical language

match, colour names (orange, light blue, yellow, light green, red, turquoise, pink, green, purple, blue), the same, different

Assessment

This activity is not related specifically to the Assessment Signposts as it is for early familiarisation.

Record of Progress:
Numbers and The Number System 2, 3.

The activities

Activity 1
Match the Shapes

1. Have ready two sets of Numicon Shapes, one arranged in order and the other scattered.
2. Take a Shape from the scattered set and ask the pupil to find the matching Shape from the ordered set.
3. Ask the pupil to compare the Shapes to check that they match by placing one on top of the other.

Activity 2
Using the Feely Bag to find the matching Shape

1. Have ready the Feely Bag containing two different Numicon Shapes and a set of Shapes arranged in order.
2. Point to a Shape that is the same as one of those already in the Feely Bag.
3. The pupil feels in the Feely Bag to find the matching Shape. Gradually increase the challenge by putting progressively more Shapes into the Feely Bag. photo 1

1

1b

Smaller steps

For Activity 1

- Collect pairs of different objects. Play games where pupils match these objects.
- When pupils can match 'real' objects gradually introduce Numicon Shapes into the games.
- If pupils have visual impairments that prevent them from distinguishing colours the emphasis will be on matching by size and oddness or evenness of the Shape. When introducing two pairs of Shapes, start with one pair of odd shapes and one pair of even shapes that are very different in size, e.g. 3-shapes and 10-shapes. Increase the variety and difficulty (similarity in size) as pupils gain in confidence.

For Activity 2

- Introduce the idea of identifying objects by touch by putting a familiar object into the Feely Bag and asking pupils what it is. Gradually increase to two and then three objects asking pupils to feel in the Feely Bag for a specific one.
- Some pupils may have an aversion to the Feely Bag, in which case, find other ways to 'hide' the Shapes so pupils have to identify them by touch, e.g. a 'feely box'.
- Introduce the matching aspect of the activity by including two or more pairs of objects and a pair of Numicon Shapes. Put one of each pair in the Feely Bag and one of each on the table. Point to one of the objects on the table and ask the pupil to feel in the Feely Bag for the matching object.
- Repeat just with pairs of Numicon Shapes. Initially work with only two pairs of Shapes of very different sizes. Gradually increase the variety of Shapes used.

Extending the activities

Connecting activities for all children

- Colour matching activities.
- Colour Dominoes.
- Colour or shape lotto.

For pupils moving on quickly

- To encourage naming colours, make a spinner overlay showing the colour of the Shapes (Photocopy Master 7). Pupils spin a colour and find the matching Shape (pupils may be able to do the activity without yet knowing colour names). photo 2
- Prepare a basket containing several of each Numicon Shape for pupils to sort. As pupils are ready encourage them to look for criteria other than colour.
- Use Numicon Software on a computer, set up a screen with sorting hoops and a selection of Numicon Shapes for pupils to sort virtually.

2

Key mathematical ideas: Pattern, Order, Space

Getting to Know the Numicon Shapes

Aims, language and assessment

Aims

To match Numicon Shapes to coloured pictures of the Shapes.

Language of instruction

feel, find, match, turn over, turn round, 'see in your mind's eye', 'see in your head'

Mathematical language

match, turn over, turn round, colour names (orange, light blue, yellow, light green, red, turquoise, pink, green, purple, blue), the same as, different

Assessment

This activity is not related specifically to the Assessment Signposts as it is for early familiarisation, though there are opportunities for developing language of size, comparison and position.

Record of Progress:
Using Pattern 1, 2, 3, 4, 5.

The activities

Activity 1
Using the Picture Overlays

1. Put out a Baseboard with one of the Picture Overlays and a basket of Numicon Shapes for pupils to match onto the Overlays.
2. Pupils can also take the Shapes one by one from the Feely Bag and match them to complete the picture. photo 1

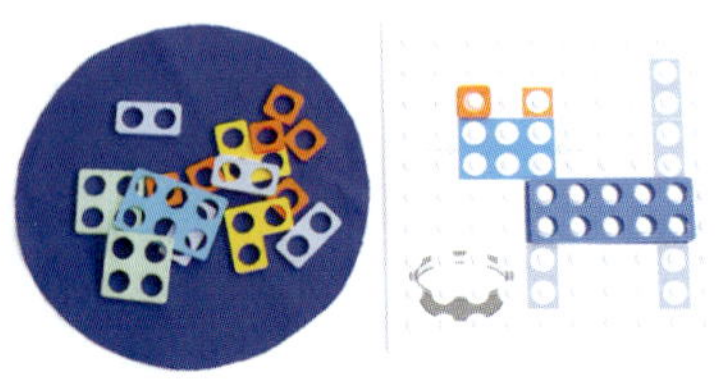

1

Smaller steps

- Prepare 'mats' each showing only one Numicon Shape, by cutting out Shape outlines (Photocopy Master 2).
- Ask pupils to match the Shapes to the mats (gradually increase the number of mats and Shapes).
- Choose one of the simpler picture overlays (Cat or Lorry) and put out only the Shapes needed.

2a

Extending the activities

Using Numicon

- Pupils match Numicon Shapes to the Cover the Board Picture Overlay.
- Pupils match Numicon Shapes to the Numicon Number Line. photo 2

Connecting activities for all children

Shape and colour matching activities:
- Dot and colour dominoes.
- Colour or shape lotto.

For pupils moving on quickly

- Give pupils opportunities to create their own pictures with Numicon Shapes both on and off the Baseboard.
- Encourage pupils to begin to visualise Numicon Shapes by putting the Shapes for one of the Overlays in the Feely Bag. Point one by one to the pictures of the Shapes on the Overlay, while pupils feel in the Feely Bag to find matching Numicon Shapes.
- Put some Shapes in the Feely Bag. Pupils feel in the Bag for a Shape and describe its size. Some pupils may have already started to use the language of 'odd' and 'even'. When pupils are already visualising the Shapes they may also say the colour of the Shape they are feeling for.

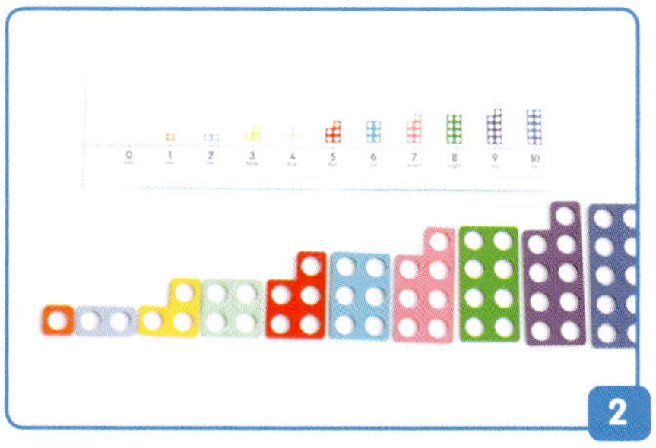

2

Key mathematical ideas: Order, Comparison

Getting to Know the Numicon Shapes

Aims, language and assessment

Aims

To understand and use the language 'bigger' with Numicon.

Language of instruction

feel, pick up, find, point to

Mathematical language

big, bigger, biggest, large, larger, largest

Assessment

Record of Progress:
Using Pattern 1, 2, 3, 4, 5.

The activities

Activity 1
Finding the bigger of two Numicon Shapes

1. Have ready a 10-shape and a 1-shape. Ask pupils to pick up the bigger one. photo 1
2. Put both Numicon Shapes in the Feely Bag, and ask pupils to feel for the bigger Shape.
3. Practise often with different pairs of Shapes changing the selection to make sure that pupils can find the bigger Shape from 4 and 6 and the bigger Shape from 4 and 3, for example.
4. Pupil takes on the role of teacher by choosing two Shapes and asking 'Can you find the bigger Shape?'

Activity 2
Finding the biggest of three Numicon Shapes

1. Have ready three different Numicon Shapes, e.g. 4, 5 and 6. Ask pupils to pick up the biggest Shape.
2. Pupil takes on the role of teacher by choosing three Shapes and asking 'Can you find the biggest Shape?'

1

2b

Smaller steps

The relative meaning of 'bigger' makes it difficult for some pupils to understand. Before doing these activities pupils may need to work on 'big' in relation to everyday objects/toys, etc. and to use 'not big' before using 'bigger'. Refer to Teaching Guide, page 16: Difficulties with the language of mathematics.

'Big' and 'not big'

- Have ready pairs of different sized similar objects, e.g. a big ball and a small ball; a big toy car and a small toy car.
- Show pupils a pair of different sized objects. Ask pupils to pick up/point to/find the 'big' object. Ask pupils to pick up/point to/find the 'not big' object.

Introducing 'bigger'

- Have ready sets of three different sized similar objects.
- To start with show pupils only the smallest and middle-sized objects from the set, ask pupils to find or point to the big/bigger one.
- When pupils can do this confidently and consistently replace the bigger object with the one that is even bigger than the 'bigger of the first two'. Ask pupils now to find or point to the bigger one.

Introducing 'bigger' with Numicon in smaller steps

Repeat the above Smaller Steps activities replacing the objects with Numicon Shapes. To start with work with the 1-shape in comparison with other Shapes, and then work with the 2-shape in comparison with other Shapes.

Introducing biggest

In preparation for Activity 2, have ready a set of three different sized similar objects/toys. Ask pupils to find the biggest one.

Extending the activities

Using Numicon

Make a fishing game, by attaching adhesive magnets to cut-out pictures of Numicon Shapes (use Photocopy Master 2). Pupils have to 'fish' for two Shapes and find the bigger one.

Connecting activities for all children

- Stories that involve the idea of big like *Jack and the Beanstalk, The Enormous Turnip, The Giant Jam Sandwich.*
- Discussion about situations with which pupils will be familiar, e.g. big balls in PE, big chairs in the classroom, big lorries, big books, etc.

For pupils moving on quickly

- Give pupils Numicon Shapes that are close in size, e.g. 6 and 7, for them to find the bigger one.
- Give pupils more than three Shapes for them to find the biggest.
- Repeat Activity 3 talking about what to call the Shape that is left (medium, middle-sized).

Key mathematical ideas: Order, Comparison

Getting to Know the Numicon Shapes

Aims, language and assessment

Aims

To understand and use the language 'smaller' with Numicon.

Language of instruction

pick up, find, feel, point to

Mathematical language

smaller, smallest, larger, largest

Assessment

Record of Progress:
Using Pattern 1, 2, 3, 4, 5.

The activities

Activity 1
Finding the smaller of two Numicon Shapes

1. Have ready a 10-shape and a 1-shape. Ask pupils to pick up the smaller one. photo 1
2. Put both Shapes in a Feely Bag, and ask pupils to feel for the smaller Shape.
3. Work with the 1-shape in comparison with Shapes 6-10 initially and then repeat comparing the 2-shape with other Shapes.
4. Practise often with different pairs of Shapes changing the selections to make sure that pupils can find the smaller Shape from 4 and 6 and then the smaller Shape from 4 and 3, for example.
5. The pupil takes on the role of teacher by choosing two Shapes and asking 'Can you find the smaller Shape?'

Activity 2
Smallest

1. Have ready three different Numicon Shapes. Ask pupils to pick up the smallest Shape.
2. The pupil takes on the role of teacher by choosing three Shapes and asking 'Can you find the smallest Shape?' photo 2

1

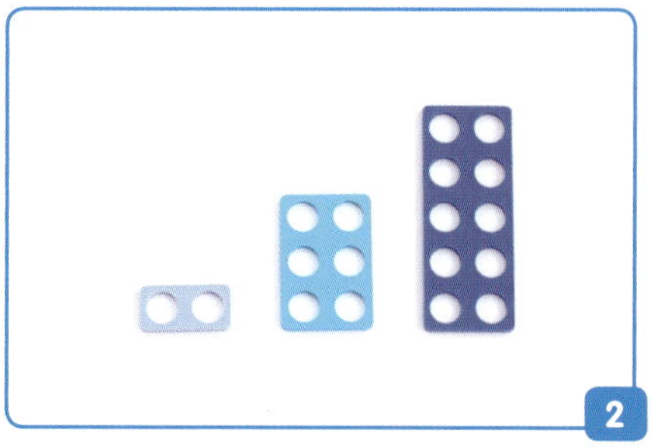
2

3a

Smaller steps

The comparative meaning of 'smaller' makes it difficult for pupils to understand. Therefore, before the activities with Numicon some pupils may need to work on 'small' in relation to everyday objects and to use 'not small' before using 'smaller'. Refer to Teaching Guide, page 16: Difficulties with the language of mathematics.

'Small' and 'not small'

- Have ready pairs of different sized similar objects, e.g. a small figure and a large figure; a small toy car and a large toy car.
- Show pupils one of the pairs and ask them to pick up/point to/find the 'small' object. Ask pupils to pick up/point to/find the 'not small' object.

Introducing 'smaller'

- Have ready sets of three different sized similar objects.
- To start with show pupils only the middle-sized and smallest objects from the set; ask pupils to find or point to the small/smaller one.

When pupils can do this confidently replace the smaller object with the one that is even smaller than the 'smaller of the first two'. Now ask pupils to find or point to the smaller one.

When pupils understand small, smaller and smallest with real objects introduce the Numicon Shapes as in Activities 1 and 2.

Extending the activities

Using Numicon

- Make a fishing game by attaching adhesive magnets to cut-out pictures of Numicon Shapes (use Photocopy Master 2).
- Pupils can take two Shapes from the Feely Bag and find the smaller one.

Connecting activities for all children

- Stories that involve the idea of small characters.
- Discussion about situations with which pupils will be familiar, e.g. small balls in PE, small chairs in the classroom, small lorries, small books, etc.
- Make a collection of very small objects (how many things can be fitted into a matchbox?).

For pupils moving on quickly

- Give pupils Numicon Shapes that are close in size, e.g. 6 and 7, and ask them to find the smaller one.
- Give pupils more than three Shapes for them to find the smallest.

Key mathematical ideas: Order, Comparison

Getting to Know the Numicon Shapes

Aims, language and assessment

Aims

To use the language of comparative size with Numicon.

Language of instruction

pick up, find, feel, point to

Mathematical language

bigger, biggest, smaller, smallest, middle-sized, medium, larger, largest, bigger than, smaller than

Assessment

Record of Progress:
Using Pattern 1, 2, 3, 4, 5, 6, 7.

The activities

Activity 1
Which is the biggest? Which is the smallest?

1. Have ready four different Numicon Shapes. Ask pupils to pick up the biggest one and then the smallest one. Encourage pupils to use 'biggest' and 'smallest' to describe what they are doing. photo 1
2. Repeat with different Shapes until pupils are confident.

Activity 2
Bigger than, smaller than

1. Have ready three different Numicon Shapes. Point to the middle-sized Shape and say to pupils 'Pick up the Shape that is bigger than this one'. photo 2
2. Repeat Step 1 but point to the middle-sized Shape, and ask pupils 'Can you pick up the Shape that is smaller than this one?'
3. Repeat Steps 1 and 2, reversing roles so that pupils are using the language 'bigger than' and 'smaller than'.

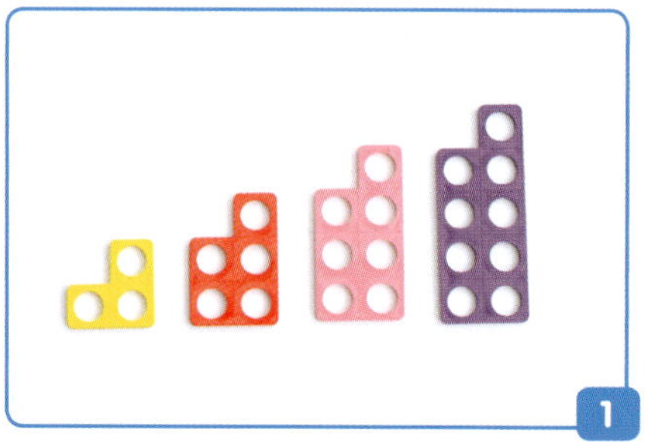

1

2

3b

Smaller steps

Prepare sets of small, large and middle-sized, similar objects. Talk about the objects focusing on their comparative size and then use them to do Activities 1 and 2. When pupils can use the language successfully with real objects repeat Activities 1 and 2, to start with using Numicon Shapes that are very different in size.

Extending the activities

Using Numicon

- Have ready the Spinner with the Pattern Overlay 1-5 (Photocopy Master 6) and a set of Shapes 1-10. Pupils spin a Numicon pattern and then find a Shape that is bigger. Repeat with Pattern Overlay 6-10 (Photocopy Master 6) and find a Shape that is smaller. photo 3
- Make a fishing game, by cutting out Numicon Shapes from card (use Photocopy Master 2). Attach adhesive magnets to the card Shapes. Pupils take turns to 'fish' for three Shapes and put them in order of size. photo 4

Connecting activities for all children

- Stories which involve small, medium and large.
- Ordering different sized and different shaped containers, including those that stack and nest.

For pupils moving on quickly

- When comparing three Numicon Shapes talk about what to call the one that is left and introduce the words middle-sized and medium.
- Extend the number of Shapes to give further opportunities for comparison.

3

4

Key mathematical ideas: Order, Comparison

Learning to Order the Numicon Shapes

Aims, language and assessment

Aims

To put Numicon Shapes in order of size.

Language of instruction

put in order

Mathematical language

first, last, next, after, before, in between

Note: Pupils usually learn 'first' and 'last' prior to learning 'before' and 'after' because 'first' and 'last' are absolute within a particular series, whereas 'next', 'before' and 'after' are relative to each particular item in the series.

Some pupils may call the Numicon Shapes by their number names, but for others the emphasis will be on size and pattern.

Assessment

Record of Progress:
Using Pattern 4, 5, 6, 7, 8, 9.

The activities

Activity 1
Jumbled Shapes

1. Have ready Shapes scattered on the table.
2. Explain that the activity is to put the Shapes in order starting with the smallest, and then show pupils what to do.
3. Jumble the Shapes, pick out the first one and ask pupils to find the next one. Continue until all Shapes are ordered.

Smaller steps

- Use a visual timetable to help pupils understand 'before' and 'after' in the sequence of their daily routines. photo 1
- Focus on one temporal concept at a time before using them together. Use 'after', and when pupils are confident, introduce the word 'next'. Then introduce 'before'.
- Use signing to support pupils' understanding of this language.
- Prepare collections of everyday objects for pupils to arrange in order of size.
- Give pupils a frame (Photocopy Master 5) to help them organise the Shapes in order. Work initially from 1-3 increasing gradually up to 10. photo 2

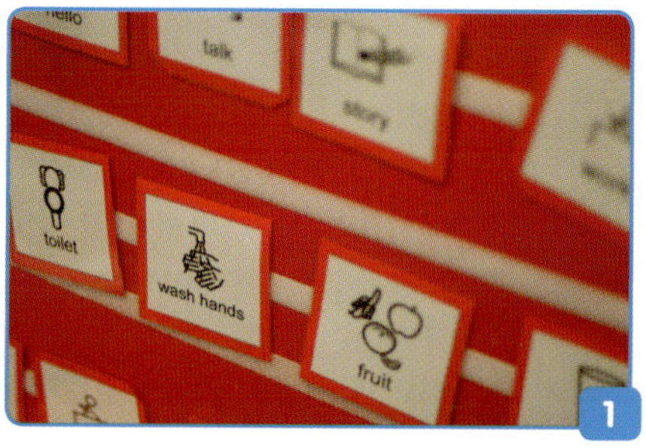

1

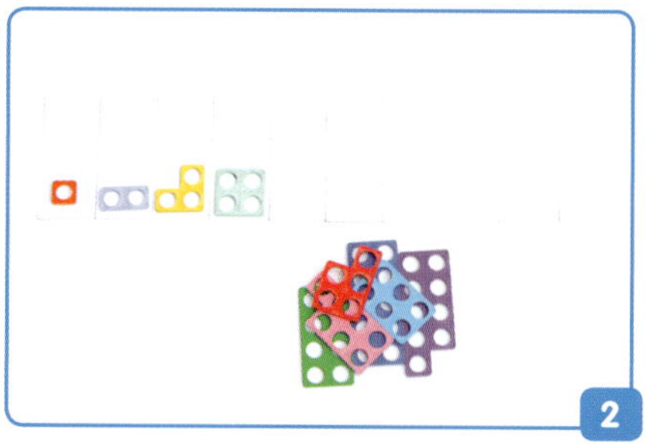
2

4a

Extending the activities

Using Numicon

- Use the Baseboard Overlay that shows coloured Shapes in order. Pupils match Numicon Shapes to the Overlay.
- When pupils are confident try the activity using the reverse of the Overlay which shows grey pictures of the Shapes in order. photo 3
- Have available a magnetic board with Numicon Shapes for pupils to order independently.
- Cut out pictures of Numicon Shapes (Photocopy Master 2) for pupils to glue onto paper in order of increasing size and decreasing size.

Connecting activities for all children

- Ordering puzzles.
- Nesting and stacking toys.
- Ordering Number Rods.
- Ordering different shaped containers, e.g. bottles.
- Songs with repeated sequences.
- Cutting out pictures of different sized objects (from magazines, etc.) to glue onto paper in order of increasing size and decreasing size.

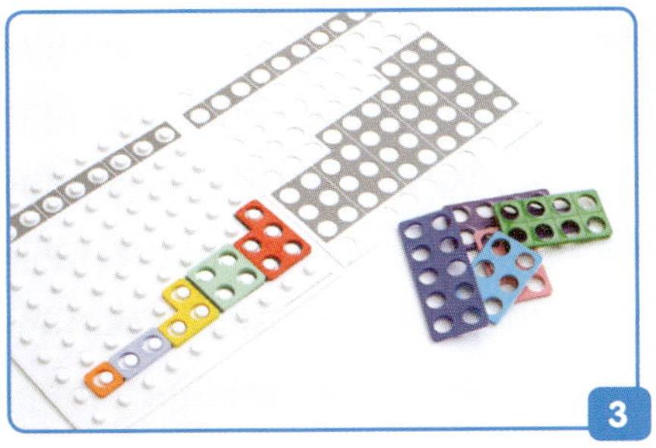
3

For pupils moving on quickly

- Pupils order the Numicon Shapes independently.
- Pupils find the next Shape starting anywhere in the series. Pupils find the previous Shape from any point in the series.

Key mathematical ideas: Order, Comparison

Learning to Order the Numicon Shapes

Aims, language and assessment

Aims

To order Numicon Shapes confidently and securely.

Language of instruction

order, arrange, swap, change over, look, find, what's wrong, put right

Mathematical language

Reinforce language of size, order and position.

Assessment

Record of Progress:
Using Pattern 10, 11.

The activities

Note: Some pupils may call the Numicon Shapes by their number names, but for others the emphasis will be on size and pattern. Remember to model the correct use of number names.

Activity 1
Swaps

1. Arrange Shapes 1-10 in order. Ask pupils to close their eyes, and then swap the order of two Shapes.
2. Ask a pupil to move the two Shapes back to their correct places. photo 1

1

Activity 2
Fill the gap

1. Arrange Shapes 1-10 in order and have ready another set scattered nearby. Ask pupils to close their eyes and remove a Shape from the ordered set.
2. Pupils pick up the Shape from the scattered set to fill the gap.

4b

Smaller steps

For Activities 1 and 2

- Have a set of Numicon Shapes 1-10 in order to which pupils can refer.
- Use fewer Shapes.

For Activity 1

- Swap far apart Shapes to start with, working towards swapping adjacent Shapes.

Extending the activities

Using Numicon

Pupils cut out Numicon Shapes from sticky paper to create their own ordered rows.

Connecting activities for all children

- Continue a variety of sequencing and ordering activities.
- Set up play situations where something is in the wrong place or position, encourage pupils to describe 'what's wrong'.
- Look at and discuss 'spot what's wrong' pictures.
- Use a sequence of pictures that tell a story, remove one picture, and ask pupils to describe 'what's wrong or missing'.
- Look at and discuss pictures that have one feature missing.

Activity 1 for pupils moving on quickly

- Pupils explain which Shapes to move and where to place them.
- Pupils describe missing or swapped Shapes. (They may use colour or number names.)

Activity 2 for pupils moving on quickly

Remove the 1-shape or the 10-shape. Increasing the difficulty by 'closing the gap'.

Key mathematical ideas: Pattern, Shape

Getting to Know the Numicon Shapes and Patterns

Aims, language and assessment

Aims

To match Numicon Shapes to grey pictures of the Shapes, outlines of the Shapes and small representations of the Numicon Patterns as shown on the Spinner Overlays.

Language of instruction

Match, spin, find, feel, press, draw, look, listen.

Mathematical language

shape, pattern, large, small, big, little, bigger, smaller, colour words, outline, order, pattern (some pupils may start using number names to describe the Shapes).

Assessment

This activity is for early familiarisation, it is linked to pupils recognising the pattern of each Numicon Shape in preparation for:

Record of Progress:
Numbers and The Number System 4, 5.

The activities

Note: Some pupils may call the Shapes by their number names, but for others the emphasis will be on size and pattern. Remember to model the correct use of number names.

Activity 1
Using the Grey Overlay

Put out a Baseboard with the Overlay showing grey pictures of Numicon Shapes, and a basket of Numicon Shapes for pupils to match to the Overlay. photo 1

Activity 2
Playing with Spinners with Numicon Pattern Overlays

1. Have ready Numicon Shapes 1-5 in order and a Spinner with the Pattern Overlay 1-5 (Photocopy Master 6).
2. Pupils spin a pattern and find the matching Shape.

Activity 3
Finding Shapes in the Feely Bag

1. Have ready a Feely Bag or basket containing Shapes 1-5 and a Spinner with the Pattern Overlay 1-5 (Photocopy Master 6).
2. Pupils spin a pattern and feel for the matching Shape in the Bag. photo 2

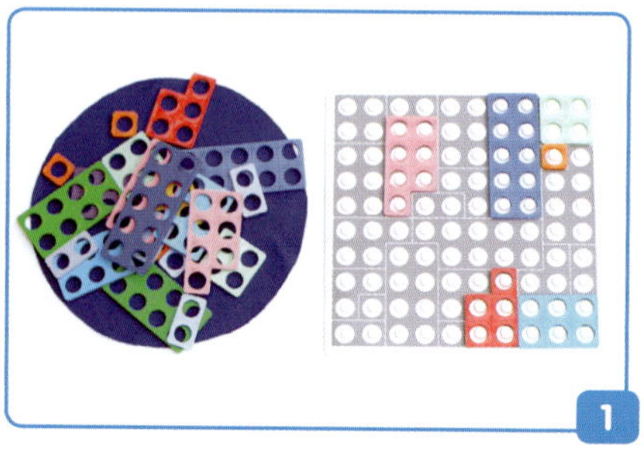

1

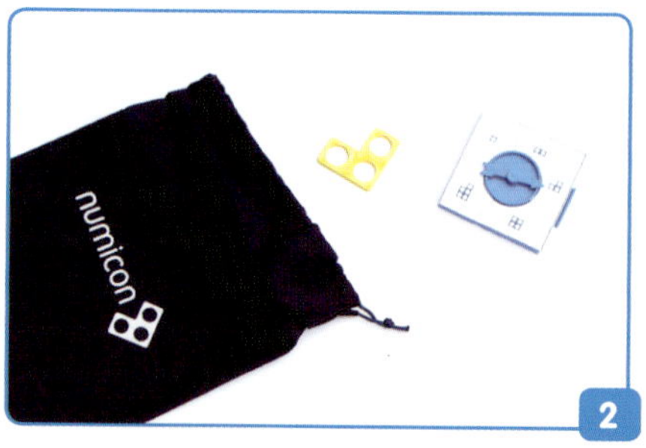

2

5a

Smaller steps

- Press Numicon Shapes into play dough or wet sand, to reveal the outline and pattern.
- Cut out Numicon Shapes 1-10 from card (Photocopy Master 2). Ask pupils to match actual Shapes to the card Shapes.
- Make Spinner overlays with Numicon patterns in colours to match the Shapes by colouring the shape patterns on the Spinner Overlays (Photocopy Master 7). Gradually introduce the Overlays with black patterns when pupils are ready.

Extending the activities

Using Numicon

- Help pupils to draw round the outline and the holes to reveal the pattern of holes. Pupils can then match Numicon Shapes to the outlines they have drawn.
- Match Numicon Shapes to the Display Number Line.

Connecting activities for all children

Activities where pupils have to look carefully at a shape, e.g. shape posting boxes, shape inset puzzles, jigsaw puzzles.

Activities 2 and 3 for pupils moving on quickly

Use both Spinners with Overlays 1-5 and 6-10 and a full set of Shapes 1-10.

Key mathematical ideas: Pattern, Shape

Getting to Know the Numicon Shapes and Patterns

Aims, language and assessment

Aims

To learn the patterns of the Numicon Shapes.

Language of instruction

look, arrange, copy, match, check, fit, put

Mathematical language

shape, pattern, the same, different, bigger, smaller, more, fewer, less

Assessment

Record of Progress:
Numbers and The Number System 4, 5.

The activities

Note: Knowing the Numicon Shapes and being able to copy their patterns shown in the arrangement of holes, is the essential basis for all the following work. Repeat this card often until pupils are secure and continue to revisit it even after they have moved on to the later activities.

Activity 1
Copying Numicon patterns

1. Have ready a Baseboard and baskets of Pegs sorted into colours.
2. Arrange Pegs into the pattern of a Numicon Shape using Pegs of one colour, and ask pupils to copy the pattern. photo 1

Activity 2
Find the Shape

1. Have ready Shapes in order, a Baseboard and baskets of Pegs sorted into colours.
2. Arrange the Pegs to make one of the Numicon Shapes. Pupils pick up the corresponding Numicon Shape and check by placing it on top of the arranged Pegs. photo 2

Activity 3
Make a Numicon pattern

1. Have ready Shapes in order, a Baseboard and baskets of Pegs sorted into colours.
2. Ask pupils to choose which colour Pegs they would like to use. Choose one Shape and ask pupils to look at it carefully, and then to make the pattern of the Shape by arranging some of their Pegs on the Baseboard. Encourage pupils to check by fitting the Shape over the Pegs.

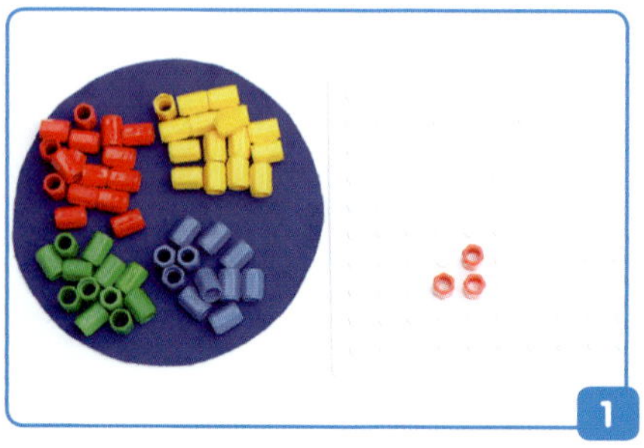
1

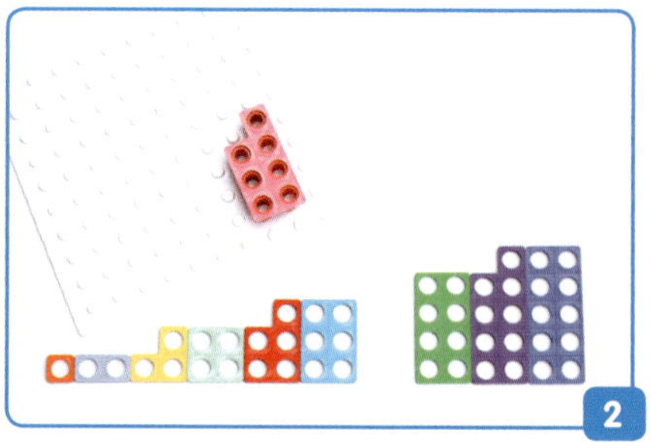
2

5b

Smaller steps

For Activities 1, 2 and 3

Work with patterns from 1-4 only; gradually extend until pupils can arrange Pegs into the patterns of all the Numicon Shapes.

Extending the activities

Using Numicon

- Print Numicon patterns with a round sponge or cork.
- Paint the dot patterns by painting through the holes in the Shapes.
- Spin a Numicon pattern using a Pattern Overlay on the Spinner and then make the pattern with Pegs on the Baseboard.
- Draw Shape outlines and colour the patterns (Photocopy Master 8)

Connecting activities for all children

- Shape puzzles.
- Collage activities.
- Give pupils 6 to 9 counters and ask them to arrange their counters in different ways or patterns, e.g. 6 could be arranged into the dice pattern, in a row, as a triangle, as a circle, etc. These arrangements can be recorded if appropriate.

Activities 2 and 3 for pupils moving on quickly

- When pupils are confident with Activities 1, 2, and 3 as described, repeat them using a mixture of Peg colours.
- Give pupils opportunities to arrange Pegs into a Numicon pattern from memory. To choose a pattern they could either feel for a Shape in the Feely Bag, or look closely at a Shape which is subsequently hidden.

Key mathematical ideas: Counting

Giving the Numicon Shapes their Number Names

Aims, language and assessment

Aims

To give number names to the Numicon Shapes and to count objects one by one.

Language of instruction

match, find, estimate

Mathematical language

how many, more, number names, enough, less, fewer, not enough, match, find

Assessment

Record of Progress:
Numbers and The Number System 6, 7, 8, 9, 10.

The activities

Note: Pupils will have been making reference to the Numicon Number Line in the previous activities, but in the activities on this card, pupils are asked explicitly to use their knowledge of the count sequence to give each Shape its number name.

Activity 1
If this is one, what's this? Giving the Shapes number names

1. Ask pupils to put Shapes 1-10 in order, starting with the smallest.
2. Point to the 1-shape, ask 'If this is one, what is this?' (pointing to the 2-shape). photo 1
3. Point to the 2-shape and ask 'If this is two, what is this?' (pointing to the 3-shape). Continue in this way until pupils have said the number name for each Shape.
4. Point to different Numicon Shapes in turn, each time asking the question 'If this is…, what's this?' (sometimes pointing to the previous Shape).

Repeat this activity often until pupils are able to name all the Shapes with confidence.

Activity 2
Fill the holes

1. Have ready Pegs and Numicon Shapes in order 1-10.
2. Pupils choose a Shape and count one Peg at a time into the holes. photo 2
3. Pupils find the matching Shape on Numicon Number Line and say the number name.
4. When pupils show confidence with this activity, ask them to estimate how many objects they will need to fill the Shape.

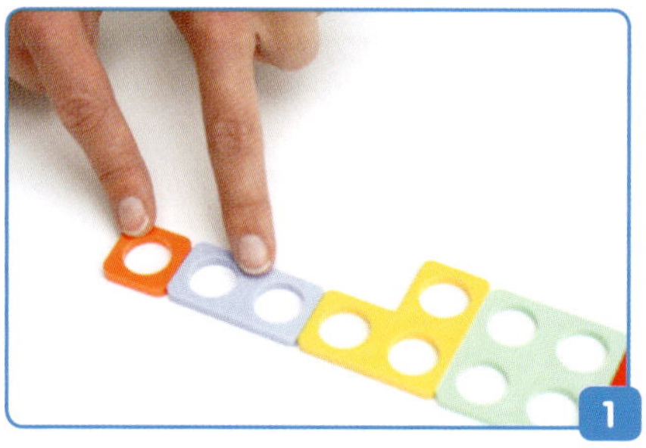

1

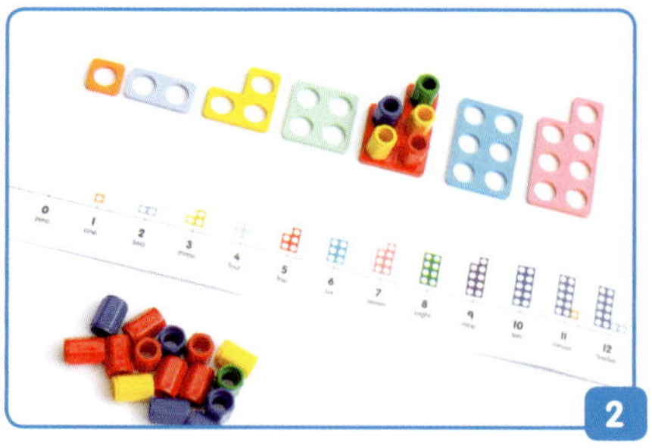

2

6a

Smaller steps

For Activity 1

- For pupils for whom analogical reasoning is too challenging, signing may help them to help them understand the question.
- Point to each Shape in turn and ask directly 'What shall we call this shape?' Reinforce by explaining when pointing to the 1-shape for example, 'We call this Shape "one" because it has 1-hole'.

For Activities 1 and 2

- Pupils who have phonological memory difficulties who are still finding it difficult to remember the count sequence, may be helped if numerals as well number names for the Shapes are introduced together. This will give them two visual prompts on which to hang their memory of the sounds of the number words.
- If necessary, initially work with Shapes 1-5 and gradually extend to include all Shapes 1-10.

For Activity 2

- If pupils have fine-motor difficulties, prepare plasticine or playdough and large card cut-out versions of the Numicon Shapes, made by enlarging Photocopy Master 2 and cutting out and laminating the Shapes.

Extending the activities

Using Numicon

- Give children other objects, e.g. 1p coins, buttons, etc. to count into the holes.
- Pupils build 'Numicon Shapes' using interlocking cubes. If appropriate these could be recorded by colouring onto squared paper (Photocopy Master 9 or 10).

Connecting activities for all children

Counting activities, refer to Counting Card B.

For pupils moving on quickly

- Children count small objects on to a number line (use Photocopy Master 3), find the Numicon Shape for the last number in the count, and check by counting the objects into the holes on the Shape.
- Pupils count out two collections each containing a different number of objects (between 2 and 10). They arrange the objects into the Numicon pattern for that number and compare the two, saying which has more objects and which has fewer/less.

Key mathematical ideas: Order, Addition, Equivalence

Knowing the Number Names of the Numicon Shapes

Aims, language and assessment

Aims

To call the Numicon Shapes by their number names with confidence and when using them in a variety of situations.

Language of instruction

match, find, estimate

Mathematical language

count, match, find, number names, how many, more, enough, less, not enough, the same as, different, next, before, after

Assessment

Record of Progress:
Numbers and The Number System 7, 10, 11.

The activities

Notes: These activities will need to be repeated many times. Continue to support pupils with phonological memory difficulties by introducing the numerals alongside the Numicon Shapes and number names.

Activity 1
Spin a pattern

A game for 2–4 players

The object of the game is for each player to collect his/her own set of Shapes (1-5 or 1-10) and put them in order.

1. Have ready Numicon Shapes and Spinners with Pattern Overlays (1-5, 6-10 or both (Photocopy Master 6).
2. Pupils take turns to spin a pattern, say the number name, and pick up the Shape to match. Before play starts decide whether players should spin again or miss a turn if a pattern is spun more than once.
3. Pupils build an ordered number line with the Shapes as they are collected.

Activity 2
Build it up

1. Pupils choose a Shape, name it, put it on the Baseboard and put a Peg into each hole.
2. Pupils then find combinations of Shapes to fit on top of the Pegs, naming them as they do so.
3. Pupils continue to build a tower, with different combinations of Numicon Shapes continuing to name the Shapes used. photo 1

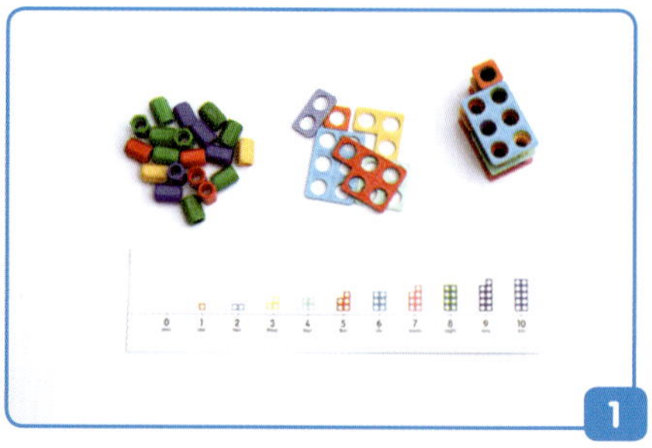

1

6b

Smaller steps

For Activity 1

- Pupils who have organisational difficulties may find it helpful to collect the Shapes and match them onto the Baseboard Overlay that has grey Shapes in order.
- Pupils may also find it easier to organise the Numicon Shapes in order by using the Ordering Frame (Photocopy Master 5).
- Work on these activities with Shapes 1-5 gradually extending to 1-10.

For Activity 2

- For pupils who have fine motor difficulties the activity can be done without Pegs, by simply placing combinations of Shapes on top of one another.
- Pupils could also make combinations of Shapes 'on screen' using Numicon software on a PC with other suitably accessible hardware.

Extending the activities

Using Numicon

- Tell or read number stories, help pupils to make connections with Numicon Shapes by using them to illustrate the number ideas in the story.
- Have ready a Feely Bag containing at least two of each Numicon Shape. Ask pupils to work in pairs and take turns to pull out a Shape from the Feely Bag and say the number name. They can check against a Numicon Table Top Number Line

Connecting activities for all children

- Ask pupils to plan their own table-top display for specific numbers.
- Refer to activities on Counting Card B.

For pupils moving on quickly

- Ask pupils to predict which combinations of Shapes they might use before building the towers in Activity 2.
- When pupils have built a tower ask them if they can recall the combinations of Shapes they have used.
- Put a collection of Shapes 1-10 into the Feely Bag, say a number name and ask pupils to find that Shape in the Feely Bag.

Key mathematical ideas: Order

Ordering the Numicon Shapes and Numerals

Aims, language and assessment

Aims

To match numerals to Numicon Shapes in order.

Language of instruction

put in order, swap, change, move, look for, read

Mathematical language

next, after, first, last, before, smaller, bigger, more, less, number names

Assessment

Record of Progress:
Numbers and The Number System
12, 13, 17.

The activities

Note: These activities will need to be repeated many times.

Activity 1
Give it a number

1. Have ready a pile of the Numeral Cards 0-10 (Photocopy Master 11) in order.
2. Pupils arrange Shapes in order 1-10.
3. Pupils take the 1-card, read the number aloud and put it under the 1-Shape. Continue until each Shape is matched with its Card. photo 1
4. Discuss that there is no Numicon Shape for zero.

Activity 2
Swap the Shape, swap the numeral

1. Arrange a set of Numicon Shapes 1-10 and Numeral Cards in order.
2. Ask pupils to close their eyes, then swap two Shapes with their numerals. photo 2
3. After looking at the new arrangement, pupils move Shapes and Numeral Cards back to their correct positions.

1

2

7a

Smaller steps

For Activity 1

Initially work only with the Numerals and Shapes 1 and 2. Gradually increase Shape numbers until pupils are ready to work with Shapes and Numerals 1-10.

For Activity 2

Initially swap Shapes that are further apart, e.g. swap the 2-shape and the 9-shape.

Extending the activities

Using Numicon

Pupils make books about numbers. On each page include Numicon Shapes, numerals, number words, collections of objects and individual details such as their age, house or flat number, etc.

Connecting activities for all children

- Go on a 'numeral spotting' walk, take photographs, e.g. of doors numbers, car number plates, calendars, scales, etc.
- Look for numerals in the classroom: in pictures, on drawers, on clocks, on calendars, etc.
- Get pupils to match numerals to collections of objects.
- Number jigsaw puzzles.
- Practical numeral formation activities, writing numerals in the air, in sand.

Activity 1 For pupils moving on quickly

Give pupils Numeral Cards 1-10 to put in order, then ask them to match the Shapes to the Numeral Cards.

Activity 2 For pupils moving on quickly

When pupils are confident with Activity 2 as shown, try swapping only the numerals. Some Pupils may be ready to extend to work with 'teen' numbers.

Key mathematical ideas: Moving beyond counting

Knowing the Numicon Patterns and Numerals

Aims, language and assessment

Aims

To practise connecting Numicon Shapes, number names and numerals without counting.

Language of instruction

turn over, match, in order, find, put

Mathematical language

number names, match, next to, between, how many

Assessment

Record of Progress:
Numbers and The Number System
14, 15, 16, 17.

The activities

Activity 1
Number the Shapes

1. Have ready Numicon Shapes 1–10 in order and a set of Numeral Cards 0–10 (Photocopy Master 11).
2. Pupils take turns to turn over a card, say the number and match it to its corresponding Numicon Shape. When the 0-card is turned discuss that there is no Numicon Shape for zero. photo 1
3. Continue until all Shapes and Numeral Cards are matched.

Activity 2
Spin a number

1. Have ready Spinners with Overlays 1–5 and 6–10 (Photocopy Master 6) and Numicon Shapes and Numeral Cards (Photocopy Master 11) spread about on the table.
2. Pupils take turns to spin a number, find the appropriate Numeral Card and match it to its correct Numicon Shape. photo 2
3. Pupils find the Shape and number on the Numicon Number Line.

Activity 3
Feel and find

1. Have ready Shapes 1-10 in the Feely Bag, and 1-10 Numeral Cards (Photocopy Master 11) arranged in order.
2. Pupils take turns to feel for a Shape and place it beside the corresponding numeral.
3. Pupils find the number on the Display Number Line.

1

2

7b

Smaller steps

For all activities

Work initially with a limited range of Numicon Shapes and Numeral Cards and gradually extend the range of numbers used. For instance, some pupils may start using only Shapes and Numerals Cards 1 and 2. Make Spinner Overlays showing the range of numbers required using Photocopy Master 7.

For Activity 3

If pupils have an aversion to the Feely Bag, the Shapes can be put in a box instead. Alternatively the ask pupils to close their eyes and then place a Numicon Shape in their hands

Extending the activities

Using Numicon

- For younger pupils roll 'ball shapes' and 'sausage shapes' from play dough and form into Numicon patterns and numerals (Photocopy Masters 12 and 13). photo 3
- Play target games where pupils record the score by picking up the Numicon Shape.
- In PE hold up a Numicon Shape and ask pupils to respond with different actions, e.g. 6 jumps, 6 hops, 6 rolls, etc.

Connecting activities for all children

- Activities and games where numerals are matched to quantities, e.g. number lotto, number puzzles, counting books.
- Count collections and label them with a number.
- Practical numeral formation activities, e.g. writing numerals in the air, in sand.
- If appropriate practise writing numerals, focusing on correct formation, through 'rainbow writing', etc.
- Refer also to Activities on Counting Cards A and B

For pupils moving on quickly

Ask pupils to match numerals to Shapes independently, and in any order.

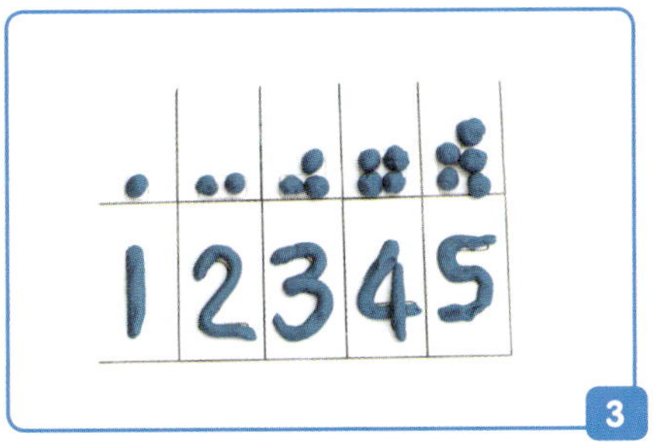

3

Key mathematical ideas: Pattern, Moving beyond counting

Knowing the Numicon Patterns and Numerals

Aims, language and assessment

Aims

To be confident about recognising Numicon Shapes and patterns, using number names and recognising numerals.

Language of instruction

match, choose, find, 'see in your head', visualise, remember

Mathematical language

number names, pattern, how many, language of size, colour words

Assessment

Record of Progress:
Numbers and The Number System 18, 19.

The activities

Activity 1
Picture the pattern 1

1. Have ready two Spinners with Overlays 1-5 and 6-10 (Photocopy Master 6), Baseboard and Pegs.
2. Pupils take turns to spin a number and say it out loud.
3. Pupils arrange Pegs on the Baseboard to make the Numicon pattern, and find the corresponding number on the Display Number Line or Table Top Number Line. photo 1

Activity 2
Picture the pattern 2

1. Have ready baskets containing different sorts of small objects or counters (e.g. shells, counters, bricks, small cars), Spinners with Overlays 1-5 and 6-10.
2. Pupils spin a number and read it out loud.
3. Pupils arrange objects to make the Numicon patterns, and find the number on the Numicon Number Line. photo 2

Activity 3
Visualising the Numicon Shapes

Have ready the Feely Bag containing a set of Numicon Shapes 1-10. Encourage pupils to feel a Shape in the Bag and describe it in their own words.

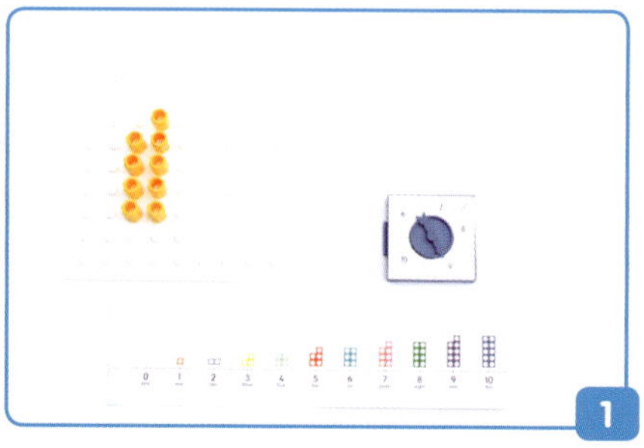
1

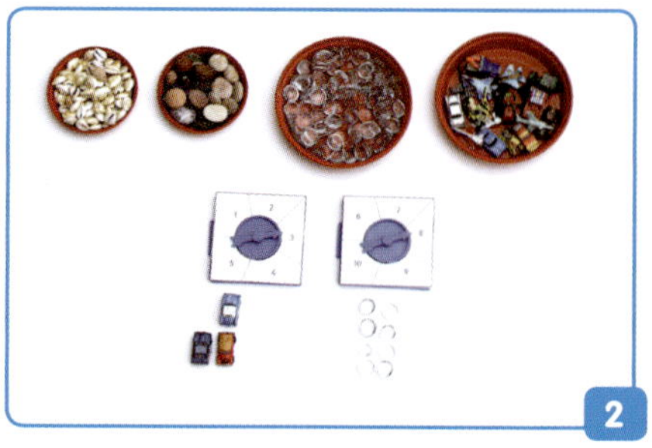
2

8a

Smaller steps

For all activities

- Some pupils may need to work initially with a limited range of Shapes eventually extending to 10.

For Activity 2

- Some pupils may like to have a frame (Photocopy Master 9 or 10) to help them organise their patterns.

For Activity 3

If pupils have an aversion to using the Feely Bag use a box or spread out the Shapes on a table top and ask pupils to close their eyes and feel for a Shape.

Extending the activities

Using Numicon

- Throw a numeral dice, collect the corresponding number of objects and arrange them into Numicon patterns.
- If you have plastic numerals pupils could generate numbers by taking them one at a time from a Feely Bag and arranging that number of objects into Numicon patterns.
- Remembering with Numicon – put out three Shapes for pupils to look at carefully, and then cover them. Can pupils remember which Shapes were there?
- Arrange stickers into patterns of Numicon Shapes and label them with a numeral. Alternatively, if their motor skills allow, pupils could draw pictures of objects arranged into Numicon Patterns and label them with a numeral. Some pupils may like to have a frame (Photocopy Master 9 or 10) to help them organise their patterns.

Connecting activities for all children

- Make connections between Numicon patterns and other arrangements, e.g. towers of blocks, number rods, domino patterns.
- Games where pupils have to remember, e.g. Kim's game and I went shopping and I bought…

Note: These games rely on different memory systems i.e. Kim's game relies on visual spatial memory and word retrieval and 'I went shopping…' relies on auditory verbal working memory. Some pupils may be able to do one better than the other. Both games may be simplified by having fewer objects or fewer words to remember.

For pupils moving on quickly

Some pupils may be ready to work with 'teen' numbers.

Key mathematical ideas: Pattern, Moving beyond counting

Using the Numicon Patterns

Aims, language and assessment

Aims

- To prepare pupils for place value.
- To see that arranging objects into patterns or grouping is an efficient way to find out 'how many'.

Language of instruction

estimate, guess, arrange, find out, check

Mathematical language

how many, patterns, groups of, tens

Assessment

Record of Progress:
Numbers and The Number System 18, 19.

The activities

Activity 1
How many without counting

1. Have ready Numicon Shapes and Numeral Cards 1-10 in order, and a Baseboard.
2. Place between one and ten Pegs randomly on the Baseboard and ask pupils 'How can we find out how many there are, without counting?' Encourage pupils to remember that they can group the Pegs into Numicon patterns to see how many there are altogether. photo 1
3. Get pupils to group the Pegs into Numicon patterns and ask them 'Can you see which Numicon pattern you have made with the Pegs without counting them?' photo 2
4. Pupils can check by placing the corresponding Numicon Shape over the arranged Pegs. Ask them to find the number on the Numicon Number Line and say aloud what it is.

Activity 2
Wrapping paper

1. Have ready a sheet of patterned wrapping paper and a basket of Pegs. Show pupils how to tally by putting one peg onto each picture on the wrapping paper. Pupils continue to put a Peg onto each picture until all have been tallied. photo 3
2. Next, collect all the Pegs and group them into Numicon patterns (first grouping tens, then the remaining Pegs) without counting.
3. Pupils say how many there are and find the numeral on the Numicon Number Line. photo 4

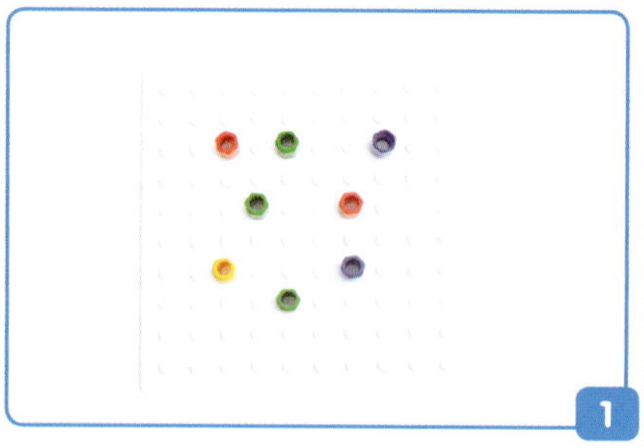
1

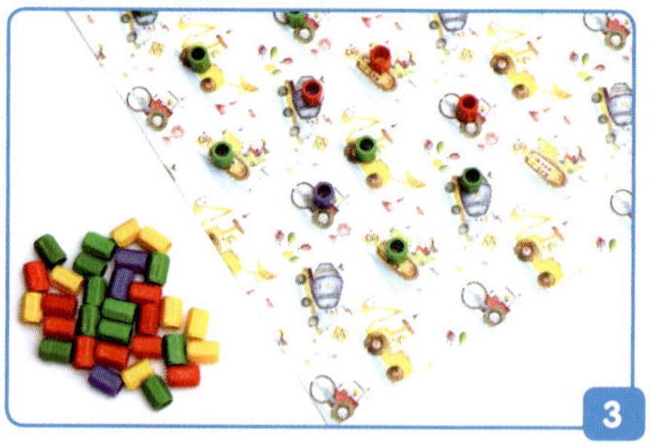
3

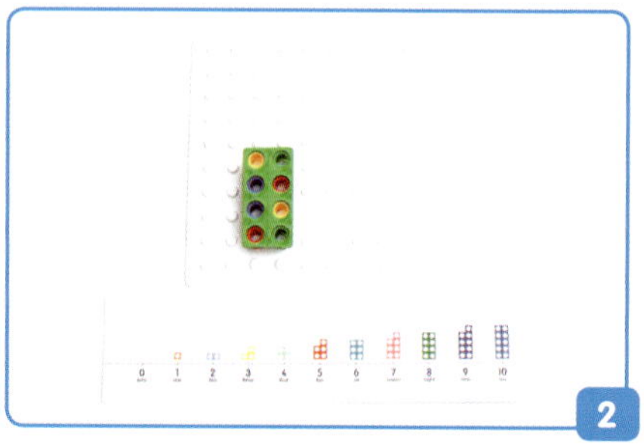
2

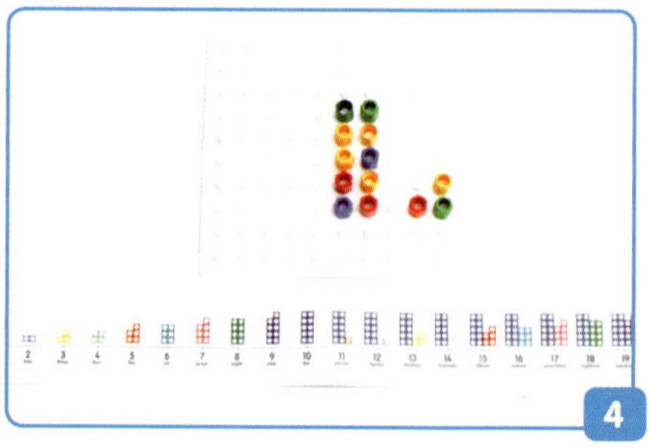
4

8b

Smaller steps

For Activity 1

Set out small collections of Pegs on the Baseboard, initially 1-4, extending to 1-10 as pupils become confident, for the pupil to group into a Numicon pattern.

For Activity 2

Choose wrapping paper with only a small number of pictures, cut down the sheet, or prepare a sheet with only a small number of pictures.

Extending the activities

Using Numicon

- Count collections of different objects by grouping into Numicon patterns (first grouping tens, then the remaining objects).
- In simple data handling activities collect data to discover, e.g. how many people in the class have cats. Ask 'Have you got a cat?' Pick up a counter for each 'yes' answer – then group the counters into Numicon patterns to find out how many altogether. If appropriate these pictograms can be recorded.

Connecting activities for all children

Whenever opportunities for counting arise, remind pupils that an efficient way to count is to group objects into Numicon patterns.

Activity 1 for pupils moving on quickly

Repeat with numbers 10-20 initially and extend if pupils are ready.

Activity 2 for pupils moving on quickly

Ask pupils to make a good guess about (estimate) 'how many' objects there are before arranging them into patterns.

Key mathematical ideas: Pattern, Moving beyond counting

Using the Numicon Patterns

Aims, language and assessment

Aims

- To use mental imagery of the Numicon patterns.
- To develop mathematical reasoning.
- To begin to use the language for addition and subtraction.

Language of instruction

remember, look, see, think, changed, imagine, find, say, explain, describe, move, arrange, hide, close eyes

Mathematical language

pattern, less, taken away from, more, added to, in order

Assessment

Record of Progress:
Numbers and The Number System 18, Calculating 2.

The activities

Activity 1
The lost Peg

1. Have ready two Baseboards side by side and Pegs of one colour arranged in Numicon patterns 1-7. Ask pupils to close their eyes, and remove one Peg from any pattern.
2. Pupils open their eyes, find/point to the pattern that has changed, and replace the missing Peg.
3. Respond and model the subtraction language saying 'I took one Peg away from… and that left…'
4. Repeat often, encouraging pupils to explain what has happened using the language of subtraction. photo 1

Activity 2
Hunt the Peg

1. Have ready two Baseboards side by side and Pegs of one colour, arranged in Numicon patterns 1-7. Ask pupils to close their eyes, then take away one Peg from the top of one pattern and move it to another pattern.
2. Pupils open their eyes, find/point to the patterns that have changed and return the Peg to its original place. photo 2
3. Respond and model the subtraction and addition language saying 'I took one Peg away from… and I have added it to the… to make…'.
4. Repeat often, encouraging pupils to explain what has happened using the language of subtraction and addition.

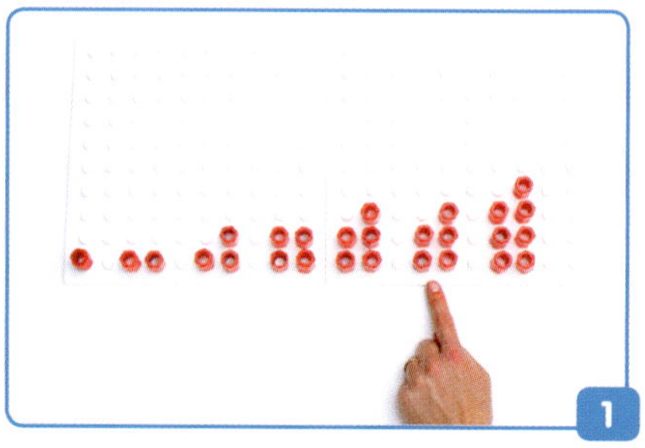
1

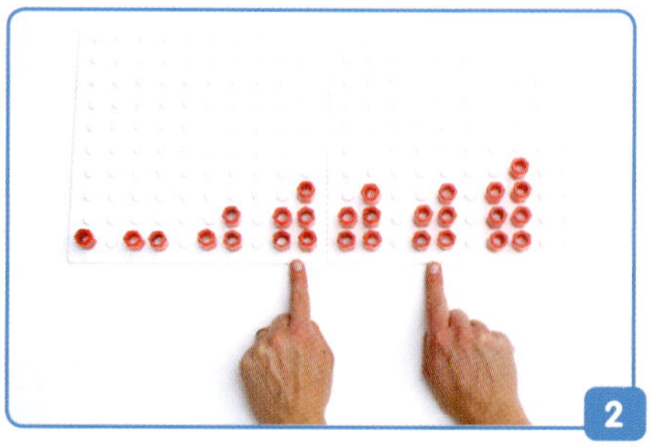
2

9a

Smaller steps

For Activity 1

Initially work only with patterns 1- 4 using Pegs of one colour for each pattern. Gradually extend the number of patterns until pupils are able to work from 1-10.

For Activity 2

Initially work only with patterns 1- 4 using Pegs of one colour for each pattern as this will show pupils clearly which Peg has been moved. When pupils understand the game, use Pegs of one colour and start with a limited range of patterns. Extend the number of patterns until pupils are able to work from 1-10. photo 3

Extending the activities

Connecting activities for all children

'Spot the difference' games.

'What's missing?' pictures.

Activities 1 and 2 for pupils moving on quickly

- Use Pegs of mixed colours for each pattern.
- Arrange the patterns on the table top without using the baseboard.
- Follow these activities with the whole range of patterns 1-10.
- Remove two Pegs from a pattern, or remove one Peg from two different patterns.

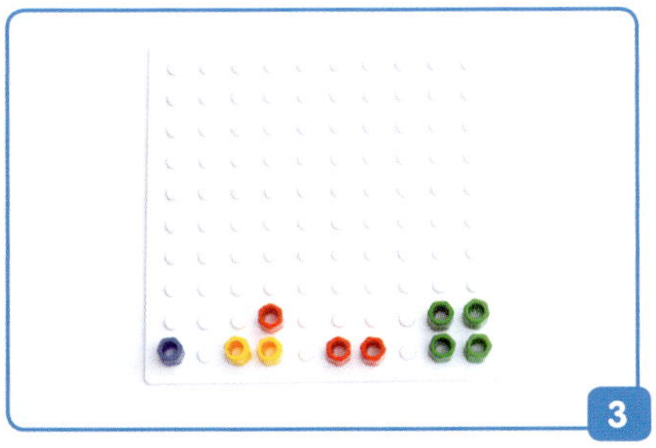

3

Key mathematical ideas: Addition

Addition

Aims, language and assessment

Aims

- To relate addition to combining two or more Shapes and to use the language of addition.
- To know that addition is used to answer 'How many altogether?'

Language of instruction

build, find, talk about, explain, put together, combine

Mathematical language

altogether, add, how many, same way, different way, makes, same number, same as

Assessment

Record of Progress:
Calculating 3, 4.

The activities

Activity 1
Numicon towers

1. Have ready Baseboard, Number Bond Overlays and Numicon Shapes and Pegs. Put an Overlay on the Baseboard and ask the pupils what they notice.
2. Pupils match Shapes on to the Overlay, thus making different combinations of the number. photo 1
3. Pupils fill the single Shape with Pegs and place one of the combinations on top. In this way pupils progressively build a tower until all the combinations are used. photo 2
4. Ask pupils to describe the combination for each layer of the tower, e.g. for the 8-tower 'four and four', 'seven and one', 'one and one and two and four', etc.

Activity 2
How many altogether?

1. Have ready Numicon Shapes and Numeral Cards 1-10 (Photocopy Master 11) in order and a Spinner with Overlay 1-5 (Photocopy Master 6).
2. Pupils spin a numeral and pick up the corresponding Shape. They spin again and pick up another Shape.
3. Ask pupils, 'How many do you have altogether?' Pupils find out 'how many altogether' by combining the two Shapes and saying the whole number sentence, e.g. 'I have put 5 and 3 together to make 8'.
3. Pupils pick up the Shape that shows the total and place it on top of the combined Shapes to check.

Activity 3
Feel and make

1. Have ready Shapes and Numeral Cards 1-10 (Photocopy Master 11) in order and a Feely Bag containing two each of Shapes 1-5. Pupils take turns to feel in the Bag and take out two Shapes.
2. Pupil combines the two Shapes and says how many it makes altogether using the language of addition, e.g. 'I added 3 and 4 together to make/equal 7'. Ask pupils to point to the numeral that shows the total.
3. Pupil picks up the Shape that shows the total and places it on top of the combined Shapes to check. photo 3

1

2

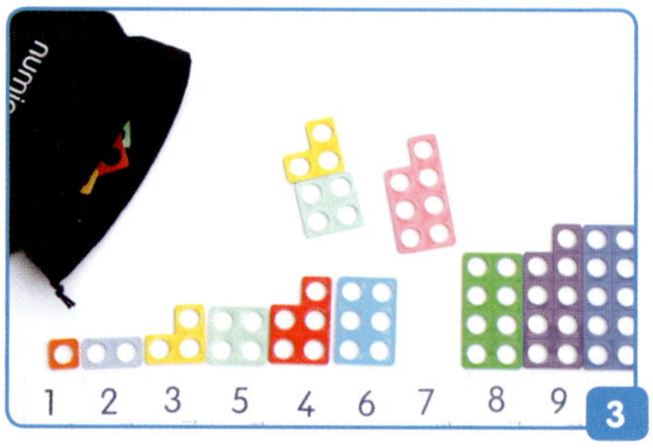

3

9b

Smaller steps

For Activity 1

If pupils have fine motor difficulties that may make using the Pegs frustrating, ask them to build towers by simply placing different combinations of Shapes on top of one another.

For Activities 1 and 2

By this stage of the teaching programme pupils have had much practice in manipulating the Shapes. However, for some rotating the 'odd' Shapes may still be very challenging. These pupils may benefit from an introduction to addition using combinations of 'even' Shapes.

Model the activities and the mathematical language before asking pupils to do them, as shown below:

- Take the 2-shape and 4-shape and say 'We can find out how many these Shapes make altogether by putting them together'. Then combine the Shapes whilst modeling the mathematical language 'I am putting 2 and 4 together to make 6 altogether' then pick up the 6-shape and put it on top to check.
- Invite pupils to try the activity and then to practise by repeating with different combinations of even Shapes until they are confident with using the mathematical language.
- Gradually introduce combinations of odd Shapes and odd and even Shapes.

Extending the activities

Using Numicon

- Exploit opportunities to encourage pupils to connect addition situations and their work with Numicon, e.g. three pupils are listening to a story, another pupil joins them, illustrate by combining the 3-shape and 1-shape.
- Ask pupils questions such as 'If we had four biscuits and five more biscuits, what can we use to help us find out how many biscuits we have altogether?' Encourage pupils to solve this using Numicon Shapes.
- Make up other addition problems and encourage pupils to think about ways of solving them with Numicon Shapes.
- Pupils choose two or more Shapes and use these to tell their own addition stories.
- Pupils could record their stories in words and pictures, including drawing the Numicon Shapes. Pupils can use the 'Baseboard' Frame (Photocopy Master 8) to help with drawing the Shapes.

Connecting activities for all children

Take any opportunities to point out addition in everyday situations. For example at snack time 'We have three green apples and three red apples, how can we find out how many apples we have altogether?' Remind pupils that instead of counting to find 'how many altogether' they can find the Numicon Shapes and put them together.

Activity 1 for pupils moving on quickly

Ask pupils to find their own combinations of two or more Shapes to fit the base Shape.

Activities 1 and 2 for pupils moving on quickly

Ask pupils to find the total on the Numicon Number Line and/or a 0-20 number line.

Activities 2 and 3 for pupils moving on quickly

- Show pupils different combinations of Shapes and ask pupils to say the addition sentence, e.g. '3 add 6 makes/equals 9'.
- Vary the language so that pupils are able to answer the question 'How many is 2 add 4 altogether?' and say '2 add 4 equals 6' or '2 and 4 together equal 6', for example.

Key mathematical ideas: Addition

Addition

Aims, language and assessment

Aims

- To relate addition to combining two or more Shapes and to use the language of addition.
- To use mathematical reasoning.

Language of instruction

say, explain, choose, check, make, put together

Mathematical language

add, altogether, more, more than, too many, not enough, number line, makes, equals

Assessment

Record of Progress: Calculating 5, 6, 7 .

The activities

Activity 1
Make that number

1. Have ready a basket of at least two of each Shape 1-10, two Spinners with Overlays 1-5 and 6-10 (Photocopy Master 6).
2. Pupils take turns to choose one of the Spinners, spin one number and read it out. (If pupils spin a '1' they have another go).
3. Pupils then make the number using two or more Shapes and say what has been made, e.g. 'I have made 6 by adding 4 and 2'. photo 1

Activity 2
Turn it over

A game for two players.

1. Have ready two each of the Shapes 1-5 in a basket, and Numeral Cards 2 –10 (Photocopy Master 11), set out in a grid, face up. The first pupil chooses two Shapes, combines them on the table, and says what has been made. photo 2
2. The pupil then points to the Numeral Card that shows the total, turns it over and returns the Shapes to the basket ready for the second pupil to have a turn. Pupils take turns until all the Cards are turned over.

1

2

10a

Smaller steps

For both activities

- First introduce pupils to the idea of selecting two Shapes that exactly cover another Shape. Give them either the 2-shape or the 4-shape and ask them to find two Shapes to cover it. Gradually introduce 'odd' Shapes.
- Pupils who have visual, spatial, and/or motor difficulties may continue to need help to flip and rotate the 'odd' Shapes when putting them together.

For Activity 1

Use only the Spinner with Overlay 1-5 and a basket with five 1-shapes, two 2-shapes, one 3-shape, one 4-shape. When pupils are confident, introduce the 6-10 Spinner and the remaining Shapes and follow Activity 1 as shown.

Extending the activities

Using Numicon

- Make up an addition problem that is relevant to the pupils you are working with, e.g. 'There were 5 people on the bus and 2 more got on, how many were there altogether?' Ask pupils what they know that will help them to work out the answer. Model if necessary by moving the 5-shape and 2-shape side by side.
- Encourage pupils to make up addition stories and illustrate them with Numicon Shapes.
- Pupils could record their stories in words and pictures and by drawing and colouring Numicon Shapes (use Photocopy Masters 2 or 8 or draw round the actual Shapes).

Connecting activities for all children

Continue to encourage pupils to use and apply their growing knowledge of addition as opportunities arise, e.g. through stories, songs, word problems, everyday situations.

For pupils moving on quickly

- Ask pupils to say which numbers can be combined to make any number from 2 -10 just by looking at the whole Shape.
- Pupils may record the Shapes they have used either by drawing the Numicon patterns using Photocopy Master 8, or by writing the numerals in the Addition circles on Photocopy Master 14. (+ has not yet been introduced so pupils should not be recording sums.)

Activity 2 for pupils moving on quickly

Introduce an element of competition whereby the first pupil to turn over a row of three wins.

Key mathematical ideas: Addition

Addition

Aims, language and assessment

Aims

- To find one more than a number from 1-9.
- To introduce the increase structure of addition.

Language of instruction

point to, explain

Mathematical language

more, more than, next, and, add, the same number as, equal to, number line

Assessment

Record of Progress:
Using Pattern 22.

The activities

Activity 1
One more

1. Have ready Numicon Shapes and Numeral Cards 1-10 in order and some extra 1 shapes. Take one of the extra 1-shapes and put it beside the 1-shape in the ordered line so that it looks like the 2 -shape. photo 1
2. Point to the two 1-shapes and ask 'What have I made?' After pupils have answered, model the correct language of addition by saying 'Yes, one more than one is 2'.
3. Continue to add an extra 1-shape to each Shape in the ordered line in turn, each time asking 'What have we made?' Encourage pupils to say what has happened each time, using the correct language.

Activity 2
Spin one more

1. Have ready Shapes and Numeral Cards 0-10 (Photocopy Master 11) in order and two Spinners with Overlays 1-5 and 6-10 (Photocopy Master 6). Pupils take turns to spin a number and point to the corresponding Shape.
2. Pupils then say what 'one more' will be and point to the equivalent Shape and numeral. Some pupils will need to continue to add the 1-shape for some time before they can do this just by looking. photo 2

1

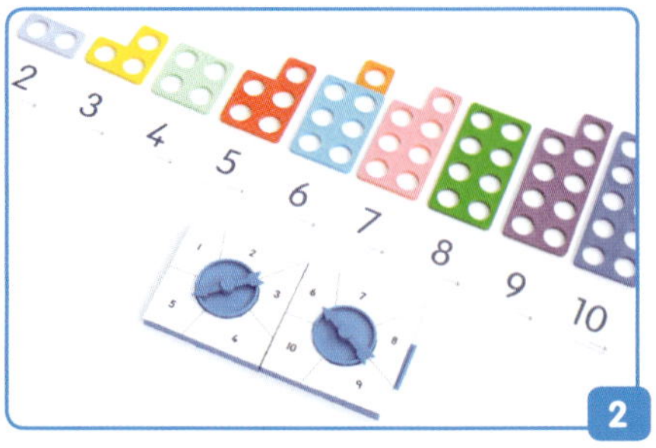

2

10b

Smaller steps

For Activities 1 and 2

If pupils have difficulty with the language they can be helped by visual prompts, including signing and displaying the number sentence using word cards and Numerals Cards.

Extending the activities

Using Numicon

- Give pupils plenty of independent practice of Activity 1. Ask pupils 'one more' questions using the Numicon Number Line.
- Play games to practise adding 'one more' e.g.
  1. Take a Numicon Shape out of the Feely Bag and add one more,
  2. Turn over a Numeral Card from a pile of shuffled 1-9 cards and add one more.

Connecting activities for all children

- Build staircases with number rods and talk about increasing size.
- Use the word 'more' in many contexts, e.g. 'We need one more biscuit.' 'Please get one more paintbrush.' 'Would you like one more turn?'

For pupils moving on quickly

Ask pupils to explain what happens when you 'add 1' to any number. Ask pupils to give 'one more' answers when looking only at the numerals.

Ask pupils to 'add 1' to any number within their counting range.

Key mathematical ideas: Addition, Pattern

Addition

Aims, language and assessment

Aims

To see doubles as special combinations of two numbers.

Language of instruction

find, cover, feel, look at

Mathematical language

pair, double, total, using the word 'double' in other contexts, compare, equals, count

Assessment

Record of Progress:
Calculating 8.

The activities

Activity 1
Doubles

1. Have ready a basket of Shapes.
2. Ask the pupils to find two Shapes that are the same to cover the 2-shape. photo 1
3. Ask pupils to find two Shapes that are the same to cover the 4-shape. Continue finding two identical Shapes to cover 6, 8 and 10.
4. Ask the pupils what they can see, and introduce the word 'double'.

1

Activity 2
Feel for the pair

A game for 2-4 pupils.

1. Have ready two (or more) of each Shape 1-5 in the Feely Bag.
2. Pupils take turns to feel for 'doubles' and find the totals on the Numicon Number Line.

11a

Smaller steps

For Activities 1 and 2

Take two 1-shapes and show pupils how to put them together. Continue with Shapes 2, 3, 4 and 5, so pupils can see the double combinations. Then continue with the activities as described.

Extending the activities

Using Numicon

Play the following games to practise doubling:

- Take a Numicon Shape out of the Feely Bag. Can pupils say what the double will total before finding the Shapes to check?
- Pupils throw a numeral dice and double the number, using Numicon Shapes if they want to.
- When pupils have completed all the work on Addition (Cards 9b-11a) they can start to find out how many ways there are of making each number from 2-10 using two Shapes. Pose a problem by asking, e.g. 'How many ways can you find of making 8 using two numbers?' They can then use Numicon Shapes to build the different combinations. If appropriate pupils may record the different ways they have found by drawing round the Shapes and colouring them. Alternatively they could use cut-out Shapes (Photocopy Master 2) which they can stick down in different combinations. Or they can record their answers in numerals using the part/whole frames (Photocopy Master 14), or use Photocopy Master 15 which gives them the opportunity to record the addition facts of each number in order to show the pattern.

Connecting activities for all children

- Pairs games
- Snap, Dominoes
- Sorting objects into pairs

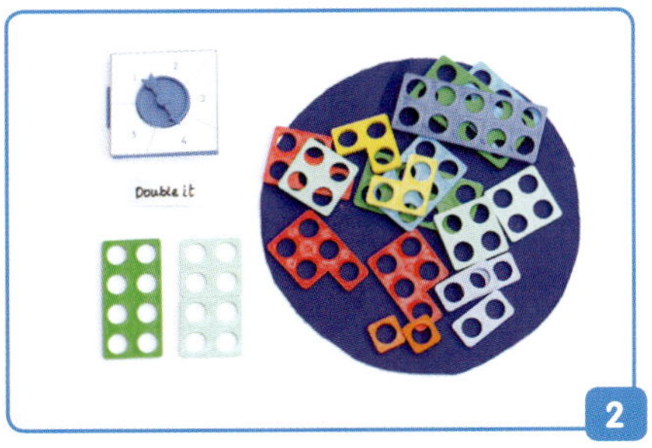

2

A game for 2-4 pupils who are moving on quickly

1. Have ready a Spinner with Overlay 1-5 (Photocopy Master 6).
2. Pupils take turns to spin a number and double it by picking up two Shapes and putting them together. The pupils say aloud the number they have made and check by covering with the equivalent Shape.

For some pupils it may be appropriate to introduce the idea of halving.

A game for 2 pupils who are moving on quickly

1. Have ready the Table Top Number Line, folded back to show 0-10, Spinner with Overlay 1-5 (Photocopy Master 6), a card saying 'double it', a basket of Shapes and a basket of 20 cubes.
2. Pupils take turns to spin a number and double it (checking with Shapes if necessary) and place a cube at the appropriate place on the Number Line to show the total.
3. Continue the game stacking the cubes one on top of each other for each double made.
4. At the end of the game the highest stack will show which double has been made most often.

Key mathematical ideas: Subtraction as Taking Away

Subtraction

Aims, language and assessment

Aims

- To relate subtraction to taking away, using the vocabulary involved in subtraction.
- To know that subtraction is used to answer 'How many left?'

Language of instruction

say, cover, check, spin, start with

Mathematical language

take away, leaves, equals

Assessment

Record of Progress:
Calculating 16, 17, 21, 22.

The activities

Activity 1
Taking away

1. Have ready a basket of Shapes. Choose a 7-Shape and ask pupils to name it.
2. Say that we want to take away 3, but because we can't break off part of the Shape we have to pretend to 'take away' by covering the part of the Shape. Cover 3 of the holes from the top of the 7 shape, asking pupils 'What is 7 take away 3?' photo 1
3. Pupils can see that 4 is left (without counting the holes) by checking with the 4-shape. Model the mathematical language saying '7 take away 3 leaves/equals 4'.
4. Repeat with other Shapes taking away different amounts. Each time encourage pupils to use the mathematical language of subtraction.

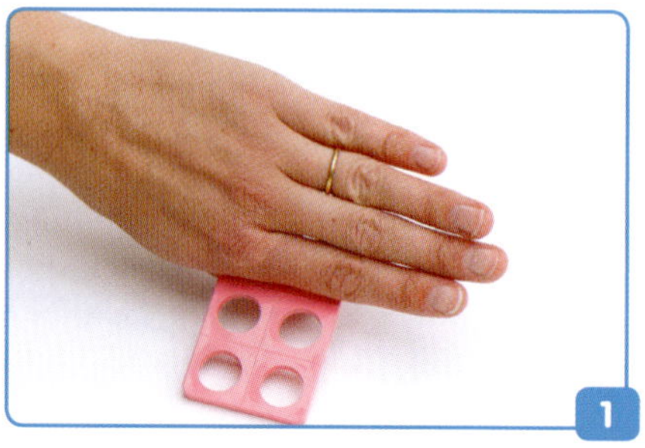
1

Activity 2
Take away a pattern

A game for two pupils

1. Have ready the 10-shape and two Spinners with Pattern Overlays 1-5 and 6-10 (Photocopy Master 6).
   The first pupil spins a number and takes away that amount from the 10-shape by hiding part of the Shape.
2. The second pupil can see the pattern that is left, says the number, and checks with the equivalent Shape.
3. Both pupils say the complete subtraction sentence. photo 2

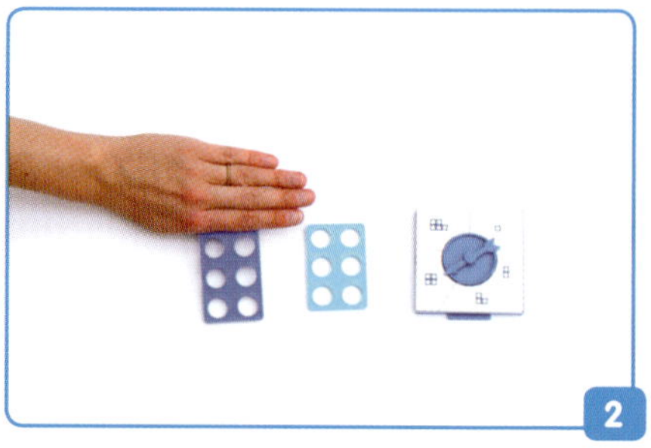
2

11b

Smaller steps

For Activities 1 and 2

By this stage of the teaching programme pupils have had many opportunities to develop mental imagery of the Shapes. However, for some pupils visualising the part that has been 'taken away' is very difficult. To help them, use the Subtraction Covers (Photocopy Master 16 and 17).

Familiarise pupils with the Subtraction Covers by giving them a set of Shapes 1-10 and a set of covers 1-10. Ask pupils to match the covers with the Shapes.

Show pupils how to use the covers to hide part of a Shape in order to 'take away', and model the mathematical language. Then ask pupils to use the covers as shown below:

- Explain to pupils that we want to find out how many are left when we take away 2 from 6.
- Take the 6-shape and say 'We can find the answer to 6 take away 2 like this'.
- Put the 6-shape on the table and place the 2-cover on the top pair of holes of the 6-shape.
- Say to pupils 'We are pretending to take away 2 by hiding it'. Ask pupils if they can see how many are left.
- Repeat the subtraction sentence '6 take away 2 leaves/equals 4'.

Invite pupils to try the activity and then to practise by repeating with different even Shapes and covers until they are confident with using the mathematical language.

Gradually introduce odd and even Shapes and covers, discussing with pupils where to place the cover. They should try:

- Taking an odd number from an odd number (cover at the top)
- Taking an even number from an odd number (cover at the bottom)
- Taking an odd number from an even number (rotate the cover to place it at the top, do not rotate it if it is placed at the bottom).

Extending the activities

Using Numicon

- Make up 'take away' stories and illustrate them with Numicon e.g. There were 8 books in a basket and 6 pupils each took one book, how can we find out how many books were left? Encourage pupils to solve these sorts of problems using Numicon Shapes.
- Pupils choose two Shapes and use these to tell their own subtraction stories.
- Pupils could record their stories in words and pictures, including drawing the Numicon Shapes.
- Pupils could record subtraction using the part/whole frames on Photocopy Master 14.

Connecting activities for all children

- Exploit opportunities to point out subtraction in everyday situations e.g. at snack time 'We have 8 boxes of juice and 3 pupils will drink a box each, how can we work out how many will be left?
- Remind pupils that instead of counting 'how many are left' they can use a Numicon Shape and cover a part of it.

For pupils moving on quickly

- After each subtraction ask pupils to find the answer on the Numicon Number Line and/or a 0-20 number line.
- Show pupils different 'take away' subtractions using Shapes, and ask pupils to say the subtraction sentence, e.g. '9 subtract 6 leaves/equals 3'.
- Vary the language so that pupils are able to answer questions such as 'How can we find out the answer to 'How many is 6 take away 2?' and 'How can we find out what is left when 2 is taken away from 6?'
- Ask pupils to work independently to choose their own Shape 'to take away from', and then say the complete subtraction sentence, e.g. 6 take away 2 leaves/equals 4.
- Ask pupils to say the answer just by looking at the part of the Shape that is left.
- For older pupils who have already met subtraction it may be appropriate to extend the language to include 'minus' and 'subtract'.

Key mathematical ideas: Subtraction

Subtraction

Aims, language and assessment

Aims

- To find one fewer/less than any number from 1-10.
- To meet the decrease structure of subtraction.

Language of instruction

point to, check, explain, arrange, take away one

Mathematical language

before, less, fewer, next, smaller than, is the same as, equal to, one less, take away one

Note: Teachers are faced with a genuine dilemma as to whether to use fewer or less, because less is commonly (and incorrectly) used instead of fewer probably because it is phonologically easier. Bearing this in mind, teachers need to decide which vocabulary they will use, and then use it consistently, at least until pupils have grasped the idea, although pupils will need to be able to use both eventually. Less should be used when comparing continuous substances, e.g. 'You have less tea in your cup than I have in mine'. Fewer is used when comparing collections of discrete objects, e.g. 'You have fewer biscuits than I'. Teachers will need to decide when it is appropriate to introduce the correct vocabulary to individual pupils, though we strongly recommend using correct terms from the start wherever possible.

Assessment

Record of Progress:
Using Pattern 23.

The activities

Activity 1
One fewer, one less than

1. Have ready Numicon Shapes and Numeral Cards 0 – 10 (Photocopy Master 11) in order.
2. Cover one hole of the 10-shape (so the 9-pattern can be seen), and ask pupils, 'What can you see?' When they have answered, model the correct language of subtraction by saying 'Yes, 1 fewer/less than 10 is 9'. The pupils can pick up the 9-shape to check. photo 1
3. Continue to cover 1 hole of all the Shapes in turn, each time asking 'What can we see?' and encouraging pupils to say the full subtraction sentence e.g. 'I fewer/less than 9 is 8'.

Activity 2
Pick and take one

A game for two players.

1. Have ready Pegs arranged in the Numicon patterns 1-10 with the Numeral Card (Photocopy Master 11) under each pattern and another set of shuffled Numeral Cards 1-10 in a pile face down.
2. The first pupil turns a Card from the pile and points to the corresponding pattern. photo 2
3. The second pupil takes one Peg away from that pattern and says what is left without counting by looking at the pattern.

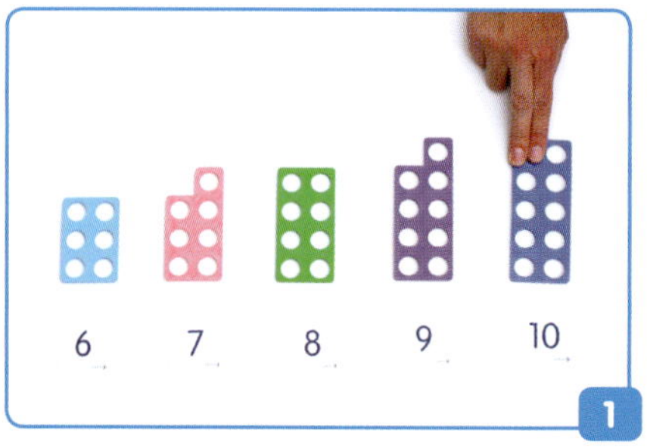

1

2

12a

Activity 3
Hide one – What's left?

A game for 2-4 players.

1. Have ready a set of Shapes 1-10 for each player and one set of Shapes 1-10 in a basket.
2. Players put their sets of Shapes in order.
3. First player chooses a Shape from the basket, hides it behind her back and says, e.g. 'I have 9, what number is one fewer/less?'
4. The player then reveals the hidden Shape and asks one of the other players 'Show me the Shape that is one fewer/less'. The chosen player responds by holding up the appropriate Shape. All the players check by picking up the Shape that is one fewer/less.
5. The game continues with players taking turns to choose a Shape from the basket.

Smaller steps

For Activities 1 and 2

For all activities support pupils' understanding of the language fewer/less by signing.

- Put the Shapes from 1-10 in order. Talk about the decreasing pattern, linking it with going down stairs.
- When covering the activities above work with Shapes from 1-5 initially, gradually extending to 10.

Extending the activities

Using Numicon

- Using the Numicon Number Line ask pupils 'one fewer/less' questions. Play the following games to practise subtracting 1:
- Take a Numicon Shape out of the Feely Bag and subtract 1.
- Throw a numeral dice and subtract 1.

Connecting activities for all children

- Pupils make up their own stories about taking away one.
- Build staircases using number rods and talk about decreasing size.

For pupils moving on quickly

Ask pupils to explain what happens when 1 is subtracted from any number.

Key mathematical ideas: Subtraction as difference

Subtraction

Aims, language and assessment

Aims

To begin to understand the comparison and difference structure of subtraction.

Note: Pupils will be familiar with 'different' as meaning 'does not look the same', but now they are learning 'difference in value'.

Language of instruction

say, compare, see, find, check

Mathematical language

difference, more, less, difference between, how many, bigger, smaller, larger, fewer

Assessment

Record of Progress:
Calculating 18, 19, 20.

The activities

Activity 1
See the difference

1. Pick up a 9-shape and a 5-shape and ask pupils what differences they can see between them. The pupils may answer that the Shapes are different colours and different sizes.
2. Explain that we are going to find the difference in size; and put the 5-shape on top of the 9-shape and ask pupils what pattern is left uncovered. Encourage pupils to use a Numicon Shape to check. Explain that the pattern that is left is called 'the difference'.
3. Model the language 'The difference between 9 and 5 is 4' and 'The difference between 5 and 9 is 4'. photo 1
4. Repeat with other examples, each time modelling the subtraction sentence, e.g. 'The difference between 5 and 2 is 3' and 'The difference between 2 and 5 is 3'.

Activity 2
Compare the spinners

1. Have ready Numicon Shapes and Numeral Cards 0-10 (Photocopy Master 11) in order and two Spinners with Overlays 1-5 and 6-10 (Photocopy Master 6).
2. Each pupil in turn spins two numbers, picks up the two Shapes, compares them and says the subtraction using the mathematical language 'the difference between'.

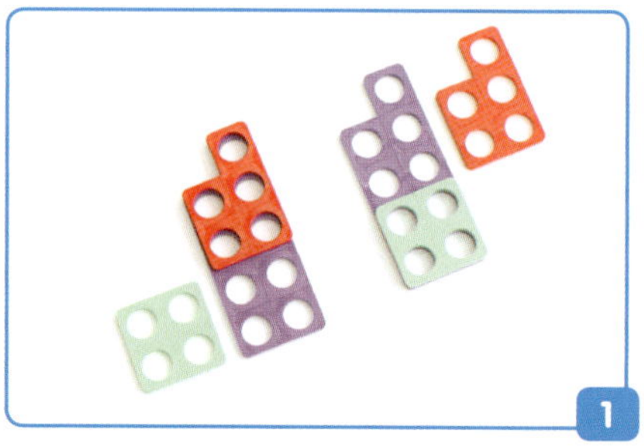

1

12b

Smaller steps

For Activities 1 and 2

The idea of 'difference' can be difficult, although it is made clear with the Numicon Shapes as described. It is not really possible to simplify this further, but pupils will need much practice over time to master this.

Pupils may be helped by the use of signing, using a different sign for things that 'look different' in the real world and finding 'the difference' in a mathematical sense.

Extending the activities

Using Numicon

- Pupils take turns to take two different Shapes from the Feely Bag, compare them and explain what the difference is using the language 'the difference between'. Give pupils plenty of practice, varying the activities by generating numbers in different ways:
- Pupils throw two dice, pick up the Numicon Shapes and compare them,
- Pupils spread out Numeral Cards 1-10 face down, turn two over, pick up the corresponding Numicon Shapes and compare them.
- Record if appropriate using the part/whole frames on Photocopy Master 14.

For pupils moving on quickly

- Ask pupils to name any two Shapes that would show a difference of one. Ask pupils if they can say the difference between two Shapes just by looking at the two Shapes side by side on the table.
- Ask pupils if they can say the difference between two Shapes just by looking when you point at two Shapes on the Numicon Number Line.

Connecting activities for all children

- In data handling make pictograms and block graphs, use the language of comparison and difference when comparing different sets of data. if appropriate pupils may record their own block graphs by colouring on squared paper.
- In measurement activities – Use language of comparison and difference in comparing pupils' heights, shoe sizes, etc. or comparing lengths of strings, ribbons, pencils, etc.

Key mathematical ideas: Subtraction

Subtraction

Aims, language and assessment

Aims

- To learn to use the language 'How many more?' and 'How many fewer/less?'
- To meet the inverse of the addition structure of subtraction.

Language of instruction

compare, say, tell, make up

Mathematical language

difference, more, less, fewer, how many more, how many less, difference between, larger, smaller

Note: Teachers are faced with a genuine dilemma as to whether to use fewer or less, because less is commonly (and incorrectly) used instead of fewer probably because it is phonologically easier. Bearing this in mind, teachers need to decide which vocabulary they will use, and then use it consistently, at least until pupils have grasped the idea, although pupils will need to be able to use both eventually. Less should be used when comparing continuous substances, e.g. 'You have less tea in your cup than I have in mine'. Fewer is used when comparing collections of discrete objects, e.g. 'You have fewer biscuits than I'. Teachers will need to decide when it is appropriate to introduce the correct vocabulary to individual pupils, though we strongly recommend using correct terms from the start wherever possible.

Assessment

Record of progress:
Calculating 19, 23.

The activities

Activity 1
How many more?

1. Pupils arrange Shapes and Numeral Cards 0-10 (Photocopy Master 11) in order.
2. Pick up a 5-shape and a 3-shape and explain that we are going to find out 'how many more is 5 than 3'.
3. Put the 3-shape on top of the 5-shape and ask the pupils if they can see how many more will be needed to completely cover the 5-shape.
4. When the pupils have answered model the mathematical language '5 is 2 more than 3'.
5. Repeat with lots more examples.

Activity 2
How many fewer/less?

1. Pupils order Shapes and Numeral Cards 0-10 (Photocopy Master 11).
2. Pick up a 5-shape and a 3-shape and explain that we are going to find out 'how many fewer/much less is 3 than 5'.
3. Put the 3-shape on top of the 5-shape and ask the pupils if they can see from the part of the 5-shape that is not covered how many fewer/much less is 3 than 5. photo 1
4. When the pupils have answered the adult models the mathematical language '3 is 2 fewer/less than 5'.
5. Repeat with lots more examples.

Activity 3
Relating 'How many more' to counting up the Numicon Number line.

1. Have ready Numicon Shapes 1-10, a Table Top Number Line folded to show 0-10, a basket of extra 1-shapes.
2. Pick up an 8-shape and a 5-shape saying 'We are going to find out how many more is 8 than 5' pupils may say '3' and ask pupils to cover the rest of the 8-shape with 1-shapes.
3. Asks pupils to check by placing the 1-shapes along the Number Line to fill the gap between the 5 and the 8. Pointing to the three 1-shapes model the mathematical language, e.g. '8 is 3 more than 5'. photo 2
4. Ask pupils to complete the connection by arranging the 1-shapes into their Numicon 3-pattern and again model the mathematical language, e.g. '8 is 3 more than 5'.
5. Repeat with different examples.

1

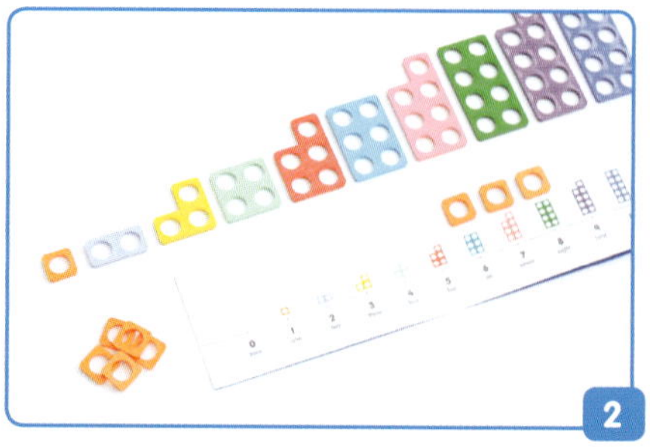
2

13a

Activity 4
Relating 'How many fewer/less' to counting back along the Numicon Number line.

1. Have ready Numicon Shapes 1-10, a Table Top Number Line folded to show 0-10, a basket of extra 1-shapes.
2. Pick up a 10-shape and a 6-shape saying 'We are going to find out how many fewer/much less 6 is than 10' pupils may say '4'. Ask pupils to cover the rest of the 10-shape with 1-shapes.
3. Ask pupils to check by placing the 1-shapes down the Number Line to fill the gap between the 10 and the 6. Pointing to the four 1-shapes model the mathematical language e.g. '6 is 4 fewer/less than 10'.
4. Ask pupils to complete the connection by arranging the 1-shapes into their Numicon 4-pattern and again model the mathematical language, e.g. '6 is 4 fewer/less than 10'.
5. Repeat with different examples.

Smaller steps

For Activities 1 and 2

On this card the emphasis is on language. Support pupils' understanding of the vocabulary by signing. Pupils are likely to need a lot of practice over time to master this.

Ensure that pupils are secure with the language of 'more' and 'fewer/less' in relation to comparing collections of objects (refer back to Counting Card and to Cards 10b and 11b).

Extending the activities

Using Numicon

- Pupils take turns to take two different Shapes from the Feely Bag, compare them using the language 'is more than' and 'is less/fewer than'.
- Pupils spin two numbers, or throw two dice, pick up the Numicon Shapes, compare them using the language 'is more than' and 'is less/fewer than'.
- Tell stories involving comparison and illustrate with Numicon Shapes, e.g. 'There were 8 pens in one pot and 6 in another pot. How many more in the first pot?' and then encourage pupils to make up their own stories.

Connecting activities for all children

- Comparing number rods.
- Comparing towers built with blocks or cubes.
- Make simple bar charts or pictograms (e.g. favourite foods, ages, pets) and use the language of how many more and how many less when comparing data.

For pupils moving on quickly, working in pairs

1. Have ready Numicon Shapes 1-10, a Table Top Number Line folded to show 0-10, a basket of extra 1-shapes, 2 Spinners with Overlays 1-5 and 6-10 (Photocopy Master 6).
2. Pupils repeat Activities 3 and 4 using the Spinners to generate the two numbers.
3. Ask pupils to say the difference between two numerals, or say how many more, or how many less, without using the Shapes.
4. Remind pupils to use their growing knowledge of addition and subtraction facts to answer.

Key mathematical ideas: Comparison, Number, Mathematical thinking

Reasoning About Numbers

Aims, language and assessment

Aims

- To begin to reason logically about numbers.
- To understand bigger and smaller in the context of numbers.

Language of instruction

work out, think, ask, question

Mathematical language

bigger than, smaller than, one more than, one fewer than, two more than, two less than, etc. before, after, between, next, odd, even

The activities

Activity 1
Describing Shapes

1. Put out a set of Numicon Shapes 1-10 and Numeral Cards 1-10 on a magnetic board.
2. Point to the 5-shape and discuss different ways of describing it, e.g.
   It is an odd number.
   It is red.
   It is smaller than the 10-shape, the 9-shape, the 8-shape, the 7-shape and the 6-shape.
   It is bigger than the 1-shape, the 2-shape, the 3-shape and the 4-shape.
   It is one more than 4.
   It is one fewer/less than 6.
   It equals 2 and 3 when they are added together.
   It is left when 3 is taken away from 8.
   It is 5 fewer/less than 10' etc
3. Repeat for other Shapes.
4. When pupils can confidently describe Shapes in many ways move on to Activity 2.

Activity 2
What Shape is hidden?

1. Have ready a set of Numicon Shapes 1-10 and Numeral Cards 0-10 in order on a magnetic board, a Feely Bag, and a basket of Numicon Shapes, and a set of Shapes 1-10 for each pair of pupils.
2. Pupils, in pairs, put out a set of Shapes 1-10 in order in front of them. photo 1
3. Choose one pupil to secretly take a Shape from the basket and hide it in the Feely Bag.
4. Say 'We can ask questions to find out which Shape is hidden in the Bag'.

   To start with pupils may ask direct questions; 'Is it red?' 'Is it 4?' Model indirect questions for them, e.g. 'Is it bigger than the red Shape?' and explain that these sorts of questions can help them to 'work out' which Shape is hidden.

1

13b

5. Help pupils to use the information gained from the answers to their questions by encouraging them to work out, 'Which ones could it be?' and 'Which ones couldn't it be?' e.g. if, in answer to the question 'Is it bigger than 4?' the pupil answers 'yes', then the adult removes the 1, 2, 3 and 4-shapes from the magnetic board. Pupils then remove these eliminated Shapes from their own sets. photo 2
6. As Shapes are eliminated the remaining Shapes show the new (and more limited) possibilities at each stage of questioning.
7. Pupils continue asking questions until they have worked out which Shape is in the Feely Bag.
8. When pupils have worked out the answer, encourage them to say 'It is the… Shape' with confidence.

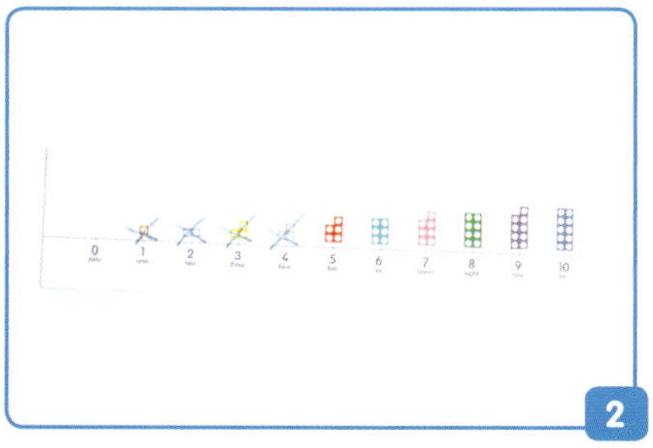
2

Smaller steps

Support pupils' reasoning by discussing the logical implications of the answer to each question.

Extending the activities

Using Numicon

- Repeat the activity with Numicon Shapes, but model different sorts of questions, e.g. 'Is the Number even/odd?'
- Repeat the activity with a set of Number Rods.

Connecting activities for all children

Activities with Logic Blocks and other reasoning games.

For pupils moving on quickly

Can pupils work out which Shape is hidden without a set of Shapes in front of them?

Introduction to the Assessment Tools

There are three Assessment Tools in this Kit. The first is Numicon Assessment Signposts, designed to help teachers identify where to start pupils on the Teaching Programme. The second is the Individual Record of Progress (page 122), designed to be used for detailed tracking of individual pupils' progress. The third (page 138) is the Pupil Profile.

Numicon Assessment Signposts
Pupils of any age and ability meeting Numicon for the first time must have opportunities to play and explore the equipment. Teachers should check that pupils are competent with the basic Closing the Gap activities (see Assessment Signposts 1-11) before using Numicon Shapes and Number Rods in Kit 1 and Kit 2 Activities. Each Assessment Signpost consists of a question about what the pupil can do and an activity which will show the teacher whether or not the pupil understands. The Signpost then indicates what should be done next within the Numicon teaching programme, depending on the pupil's response.

Working through the Assessment Signposts will help teachers identify gaps in pupils' understanding. Some pupils may appear competent at some isolated aspects of the programme but it is important that they are not moved on too far until the gaps are plugged. For example, a pupil may be able to call Numicon Shapes by their number names and assign numerals to them but be unable to create repeating patterns. As the ability to sequence is a key skill for mathematics it would be important for the pupil to develop this skill before moving on. The Signposts cover Numicon Firm Foundations Kit, Closing the Gap with Numicon (the Kit for pupils of any age experiencing difficulty with basic number ideas) and Numicon Kit 1 in which place value, equivalence, basic addition and subtraction facts and developing arithmetic strategies beyond counting are addressed. Misconceptions around these key ideas are often the root cause of difficulty for many older pupils, so each Signpost is important. When pupils have understanding of the activities in Kit 1, they have the foundation of understanding to be able to tackle the work in Kit 2. As they work through the Kit 2 programme, their understanding can be assessed using the Key questions shown on each card.

The Assessment Signposts are not designed to be a comprehensive assessment for pupils with special needs, although they will show teachers where to start these pupils on the teaching programme. The Record of Progress will help teachers to identify smaller steps within each Signpost to plan and set targets.

Assessment Tool 1: Assessment Signposts

1. Can pupil match Shapes and copy the pattern of a Shape with Pegs on the Baseboard?

How to find out

- Show pupil a 7-shape and ask him/her to make the corresponding pattern with Pegs on the Baseboard.
- Make a 9-pattern with Pegs on the Baseboard and ask pupil to find the corresponding Shape.

Yes? Move on to next question

No? Go to the activity from the relevant Numicon kit:

Firm Foundations: 2a, 2b, 3a, 5a, 6a

Closing the Gap: 1, 2a, 5

Old Foundation Cards: 1-2

2. Can pupil copy a repeating pattern?

How to find out

- Make yellow red yellow red (at least five repeats) repeating pattern with Pegs on the Numicon Baseboard.
- Ask pupil to copy the pattern on the Baseboard.

Yes? Move on to next question

No? Go to the activity from the relevant Numicon kit:

Firm Foundations: 5b

Closing the Gap: Pattern Card

Old Foundation Cards: 2a Making Connections

3. Can pupil continue a repeating pattern?

How to find out

- Make a blue green blue green repeating pattern (three repeats) with the Pegs on the Numicon Baseboard.
- Ask pupil to continue the pattern.

Yes? Move on to next question

No? Go to the activity from the relevant Numicon kit:

Firm Foundations: 5b

Closing the Gap: Pattern Card

Old Foundation Cards: 2a Making Connections

4. Can pupil order Shapes and give them number names?

How to find out

- Give pupil a set of jumbled 1-10 Shapes. Ask pupil to put them in order starting with the 1-shape.
- Point to a 6-shape ask pupil to say its number name. Continue to ask him/her to name each Shape (not in order).

Yes? Move on to next question

No? Go to the activity from the relevant Numicon kit:

Firm Foundations: 3b, 4a, 4b, 6b, 7a

Closing the Gap: 2b, 3a, 3b, 4a, 4b, 6

Old Foundation Cards: 3, 4

5. Can pupil attach numerals to Numicon Shapes and patterns without counting?

How to find out

- Scatter Shapes 1-10 on table.
- Give pupil a set of shuffled 1-10 Numeral Cards. Ask him/her to put each Numeral Card on its corresponding Shape.

Yes? Move on to next question

No? Go to the activity from the relevant Numicon kit:

Firm Foundations: 7b, 8a, 8b

Closing the Gap: 7

Old Foundation Cards: 5, 6

6. Can pupil build each Numicon pattern (without counting) in response to both hearing the number word and seeing the numeral?

How to find out

- Show pupil the numeral 8 and ask him/her to build the corresponding pattern.
- Say '10' and ask pupil to build the corresponding pattern.

Yes? Move on to next question

No? Go to the activity from the relevant Numicon kit:

Firm Foundations: 8b, 9a

Closing the Gap: 8

Old Foundation Cards: 8, 7

7. Can pupil devise his/her own repeating patterns with Pegs?

How to find out

- Give pupil a basket of mixed Pegs and ask him/her to make a repeating pattern e.g. red, blue, red, blue, red, blue etc.

Yes? Move on to next question

No? Go to the activity from the relevant Numicon kit:

Firm Foundations: 5b

Closing the Gap: Pattern Card

Old Foundation Cards: 2a Making Connections

8. Can pupil combine the Shapes to show addition and explain using the words 'add, plus and equals'?

How to find out

- Give pupil a 3 and a 4-shape and ask him/her to add them together and say the addition. Pupil should answer clearly 'three add four makes/equals seven'.
- Ask pupil to make up an addition story using 3 and 4.
- Ask pupil to show the Shapes needed to solve the problem 'There were six cars in the car park, two more cars were driven in, how many cars in the car park altogether?'

Yes? Move on to next question

No? Go to the activity from the relevant Numicon kit:

Firm Foundations: 10, 11b

Closing the Gap: 9b, 10a, 11a

Old Foundation Cards: 9, 10b

9. Can pupil show 'take away' subtraction by hiding part of a Shape?

Can pupil show 'difference' subtraction?

Can pupil use the 'inverse-of-addition' to add on to reach a target number?

How to find out

- Give pupil a 9-shape ask him/her to 'take away' three and say the subtraction. Pupil should hide the three Numicon pattern of the 9-Shape and answer clearly 'nine take away three leaves/equals six'.
- Ask pupil to make up a subtraction story using 9 and 3.
- Ask pupil to use Numicon to show the subtraction 'There were six apples in a basket, three were eaten, how many were left?'
- Give pupil a 2-shape and a 10-shape and ask him/her to find the difference and say it. S/he should cover part of the 10-shape with the 2-shape and answer clearly 'the difference between 10 and 2 is/equals 8' or 'the difference between 2 and 10 is/equals 8'.
- Ask pupils to solve the subtraction 'if you have 6 cups and you want 9, how many more cups do you need?'

Yes? Move on to next question

No? Go to the activity from the relevant Numicon kit:

Firm Foundations: 12, 13

Closing the Gap: 11b, 12a, 12b, 13a

Old Foundation Cards: 11, 12

10. Can pupil say the number that would be one more and one less of any number from 1-10?

How to find out

- Show pupil any Numicon Shape from 1-10 and ask him/her what 'one more' would be/equal, what 'one less' would be/equals. Pupil should answer by saying each number. Check all numbers up to 10. Use knowledge of pupil's understanding to decide whether to ask 'one less than one' and 'one more than ten'.

Yes? Move on to next question

No? Go to the activity from the relevant Numicon kit:

Firm Foundations: 11a (one more), 12b (one less)

Closing the Gap: 10b (one more), 12a (one less)

Old Foundation Cards: 10a (one more), 11b (one less)

11. Can pupil count accurately to at least 20?

How to find out

- Give pupil a basket of thirty five objects and ask him/her to count them. S/he should count accurately one to one to at least 20.

Note: Before starting the place value work on Kit 1 Numbers and the Number System Card 3B pupil should count accurately to at least 30.

Yes? Move on to next question

No? Go to the activity from the relevant Numicon kit:

Firm Foundations: 1

Closing the Gap: Counting Card

Kit 1, Numbers and the Number System Cards: 1A and 1B (Give daily counting opportunities supported with number lines).

12. Can pupil devise a repeating pattern using any non-mathematical objects and record by drawing or colouring?

How to find out

- Ask pupil to make a repeating pattern from a choice of objects (e.g. shells, buttons, leaves, toy cars) and then record their pattern.
- Ask pupil to make a repeating pattern with sounds and/or actions.

Yes? Move on to next question

No? Go to:

Kit 1: Using Pattern 1a

13. Can pupil use coloured cubes to devise a repeating pattern which includes quantity and record with numerals?

How to find out

- Ask pupil to build a pattern from a selection of coloured cubes. The pattern must use different amounts, e.g. 1 red, 2 blues, 3 yellows, 1 red, 2 blues, 3 yellows.
- Ask pupil to record the pattern by colouring on squared paper and then to assign a series of numbers to the pattern e.g. 1, 2, 3, 1, 2, 3, etc.

Yes? Move on to next question

No? Go to:

Kit 1, Using Pattern, 2a

14. Can pupil write an addition using + = when given two Shapes?

How to find out

- Give pupil a 3-shape and a 7-shape and ask him/her to write the sum and answer. S/he should write 3 + 7 = 10, or 7 + 3 = 10.

Yes? Move on to next question

No? Check Assessment Signpost 8 above, If pupil can demonstrate language of addition go to:

Kit 1, Calculating Cards 1A, 1B, 2A and 2B.

15. Can pupil write a sum in response to an addition story?

How to find out

- Ask pupil to write the sum to solve the problem: 'Two children were playing on the swings, three were playing on the slide. How many children were playing? S/he should write 2 + 3 = 5 or 3 + 2 = 5.
- Ask pupil to make up his/her own story from the sum 1 + 7 = 8

Yes? Move on to next question

No? Check Assessment Signpost 8 above, If pupil can demonstrate language of addition go to:

Kit 1: Calculating Cards 1A, 1B, 2A and 2B.

16. Can pupil write a subtraction using – and = in response to a subtraction shown with Numicon?

How to find out

- Give pupil a 7-shape and ask 'Please can you show 7 take away 2 and write the subtraction?'. Pupil should hide 2 of the 7-shape and write 7 – 2 = 5.

Yes? Move on to next question

No? Check Assessment Signpost 9 above, if pupil can demonstrate language of subtraction go to:

Kit 1: Calculating Cards 2A, 2B, 3A

17. Can pupil write a subtraction in response to a story?

How to find out

- Ask pupil to write the subtraction to solve the problem 'There were eight flowers in the garden, a child came along and picked seven of them, how many flowers were left?'. S/he should write 8 – 7 = 1.
- Ask pupil to make up his/her own story from the subtraction 10 – 4 = 6.

Yes? Move on to next question

No? Check Assessment Signpost 9 above, If pupil can demonstrate language of subtraction go to:

Kit 1: Calculating Cards 2A, 2B, 3A

18. Can pupil systematically build and record addition facts of any number to 10?

How to find out

- Ask pupil to build addition facts of 7 with Numicon or Number Rods and record as sums. Pupil should build facts in order starting with 1 + 6. Where pupil is working haphazardly rather than systematically s/he will need more work on sequence.

Can pupil systematically take apart addition facts of any number to 10 built with Numicon Shapes, and record as subtraction facts?

How to find out

- Ask pupil to build addition facts of 8, in order starting with 1, using either Numicon Shapes or Number Rods. Then ask him/her to show subtraction facts of 8 by taking the pattern apart and recording the subtractions. Pupil should work systematically, where s/he is working haphazardly s/he will need more work on sequence.

Yes? Move on to next question

No? Go to the activity from the relevant Numicon kit:

Kit 1: Using Pattern 2a, 3a, 4a (building addition facts)

Kit 1: Using Pattern 3b, 4b (taking apart addition facts)

19. Does pupil have confident mental recall ± of all numbers within 10?

How to find out

- Ask pupil to answer orally from reading additions and subtractions on Kit 1 Photocopy Masters, sheets 8-11.
- Read additions and subtractions aloud from Kit 1 Photocopy Masters, sheets 8-11. Ask pupil to say the answers.

Yes? Move on to next question

No? Go to the activity from the relevant Numicon kit:

Kit 1: Calculating 4a-8b

20. Does pupil have secure understanding of place value?

How to find out

- Show pupil several 2-digit numbers 15, 39, 43, 50, 81 (from 0-100 Number Card Pack in Kit 1) ask him/her to read them. Then ask pupil to build the numbers with Numicon.
- Say several 2-digit numbers (13, 28, 60, 82) one at a time and ask pupil to write them.
- Put out Numicon Shapes to show 35 and ask pupil to write the number

Yes? Move on to next question

No? Go to the activity from the relevant Numicon kit:

Kit 1: Numbers and the Number System 2a-7a

21. Can pupil add or subtract 10 from any 2-digit number?

How to find out

- Show pupil 47 (from 0-100 Number Card Pack in Kit 1) and ask him/her 'What would 10 more than this number be?' S/he should answer 57. Then ask him/her 'What would 10 less than this number (showing Number card 47) be?' S/he should answer 37.
- Ask pupil to make up an arithmetic story from 47 + 10 = 57, or 47 – 10 = 37.
- Assess pupil's understanding of addition and subtraction of 10 with teen numbers by repeating the assessment questions above substituting 18 for 47.

Yes? Move on to next question

No? Go to the activity from the relevant Numicon kit:

Kit 1: Numbers and the Number System 7b

22. Can pupil count in the fives sequence with understanding?

How to find out

- Ask pupil to count in fives whilst putting Numicon 5-shapes on the Numicon Tens Number Line.
- Ask pupil to point or highlight the 5 sequence on a number line whilst s/he counts in fives. Ask pupil to point or highlight the 5 sequence on a number square whilst s/he counts in fives.
- Ask pupil to continue the written sequence 5, 10, 15.

Yes? Move on to next question

No? Go to the activity from the relevant Numicon kit:

Kit 1: Using Pattern 5b

23. Can pupil recall facts of 10 when solving 3-digit addition?

How to find out

- Write additions: 6 + 7 + 4 , 5 + 7 + 3. Ask pupil how s/he would solve them. S/he should answer that s/he knows 6 + 4 = 10 and that 10 + 7 = 17.
- Repeat for the second example.

Yes? Move on to next question

No? Go to the activity from the relevant Numicon kit:

Kit 1: Calculating 7b, 9a

24. Can pupil use recall of facts of all numbers to 10 and his/her understanding of place value to solve ± problems mentally?

How to find out

- Write the following additions and subtractions: 40 + 30 = , 60 – 20 = , 64 + 4 = , 57 – 3 = , 52 + 8 = , 70 – 5 =
- Ask pupil to write the answers, sit with him/her to observe his/her ease of recall.

Yes? Move on to next question

No? Check Assessment Signpost 20 above, If pupil can demonstrate competency with place value go to:

Kit 1: Calculating 8b, 11a, 11b, 12a, 12b, Using Pattern 6a, 6b

25. Can pupil bridge through 10 using addition or subtraction of a single digit?

How to find out

- Ask pupil how s/he would solve 8 + 6. Expect the answer that the 6 can be split into 2 (to reach 10) and 4 more to reach 14. Be aware however that some pupils may use a different strategy.
- Ask pupil how s/he would solve 13 – 5. Expect the answer that the 5 can be split into 3 (to subtract down to 10) and 2 less down to 8.

Yes? Pupil is now ready to begin Kit 2. Whilst working through Kit 2, assess pupil's understanding using the Key Questions shown on each card and set word problems which require pupil to use each strategy as it is learnt.

No? Go to the activity from the relevant Numicon kit:

Kit 1: Calculating 13a, 13b

Assessment Tool 2: Individual Record of Progress

The Individual Record of Progress, designed to be photocopied for use with individual pupils, shows the small detailed steps of the full Numicon teaching programme, up to and including the teaching activities in Kit 2. It is arranged in three sections which relate to the three strands of the teaching programme Numbers and The Number System, Using Pattern and Calculating.

Numbers and The Number System
This section includes recognition of Numicon Shapes, knowing the Numicon Patterns, Counting and Place value. We suggest that teachers regularly assess pupil's counting until they are secure in the count sequence. This may be done by first asking the pupil how far s/he can count. Then choosing a number within the pupil's counting range and asking him/her to count on from that number and back from that number. Repeat with three or four different numbers from within the counting range. It is worth bearing in mind that when pupils are learning to count multiples of ten are common sticking points. Once pupils have counted across a multiple of ten the pattern helps them to remember the next part of the count sequence.

Using Pattern
Includes copying, continuing and creating repeating patterns, order, beginning algebra, patterns of similar calculations and number sequences. There are many detailed steps in this section because the ability to understand and use pattern is a key skill for learning mathematics.

It may not be necessary to check every step in the later number sequences but we have included them to give teachers ideas about the different sequences that pupils need to practise.

Calculating
This section covers the operations of addition, subtraction, multiplication and division. The steps within each arithmetic operation include practical arithmetic; learning the appropriate mathematical language; introducing signs; recording and using and applying.

Using the Record of Progress
We suggest that the Record of Progress is used where individual pupil's progress needs to be closely monitored. Progress will need to be tracked through the three sections in parallel. The steps within each section are numbered consecutively.

The Record of Progress is also useful as a general guide when planning. It is also worth referring to the Key Mathematical Ideas sections in the Teaching Guides which indicate difficulties that pupils may encounter.

Name: Date of birth:

Numbers and the Number System

Recognition of Shapes, counting and place value

Pupil is able to	Comments
1. Recite numbers to…	
2. Match Numicon Shapes by colour.	
3. Recognise Numicon Shapes by colour.	
4. Find Numicon Shape to match Numicon pattern built with Pegs on Base Board 1 2 3 4 5 6 7 8 9 10. (do not use number names with the pupil yet, see later steps.)	
5. Build Numicon pattern with Pegs on Base Board in response to seeing the Numicon Shape 1 2 3 4 5 6 7 8 9 10 (do not use number names with the pupil yet, see later steps).	
6. Count objects to… (note pupil's one-to-one counting range)	
7. Recognise numbers within stories and rhymes.	
8. Compare two Shapes and say which has more holes and which has fewer/less holes.	
9. Find position of Numicon Shape on Numicon Number Line by matching.	
10. Find Numicon Shape in response to hearing the number name 1 2 3 4 5 6 7 8 9 10.	
11. Name Numicon Shapes 1 2 3 4 5 6 7 8 9 10 (pupil says number name in response to seeing Shape).	
12. Recognise numerals (pupil points to numeral in response to hearing the number name) 1 2 3 4 5 6 7 8 9 10.	
13. Name numerals (pupil says number name when shown numerals – out of order) 1 2 3 4 5 6 7 8 9 10.	
14. Remove 2 objects from a set of 10.	

Recognition of Shapes, counting and place value, continued

Pupil is able to	Comments
15. Remove 5 objects from a set of 10.	
16. Remove 9 objects from a set of 10.	
17. Match numerals and Numicon Shapes together 1 2 3 4 5 6 7 8 9 10.	
18. Find out how many to 10 without counting (by arranging into Numicon patterns) 1 2 3 4 5 6 7 8 9 10.	
19. Find the last number in a count to 10 on Numicon Number Line.	
20. Begin to write numerals 1-10.	
21. Use counting confidently in different situations.	
22. Match Number Rods by colour.	
23. Recognise Number Rods by colour.	
24. Find Number Rods in response to hearing the number name 1 2 3 4 5 6 7 8 9 10.	
25. Name Number Rods (pupil says number name in response to seeing Rod) 1 2 3 4 5 6 7 8 9 10.	
26. Count on from any number within counting range (teacher establishes counting range by asking pupil how far s/he can count and then chooses a number to count on from).	
27. Say which is larger/smaller when looking at 2 numerals within 10.	
28. Find last number in a count to 10 on a number line.	
29. Record last number in a count to 10.	

Recognition of Shapes, counting and place value, continued

Pupil is able to	Comments
30. Put a list of 4 random numerals within 10 in order.	
31. Recall '1 more' than all numbers to 10.	
32. Recall '1 more' than any number within counting range.	
33. Count back from any number within counting range (teacher establishes counting range by asking pupil how far s/he can count and then chooses a number to count back from).	
34. Recall '1 less' than all numbers to 10.	
35. Recall '1 less' than any number within counting range.	
36. Count objects accurately to 30 (one-to-one).	
37. Recognise teen numerals (pupil points to numeral in response to hearing number name – not in order) 11 12 13 14 15 16 17 18 19 20.	
38. Name numerals (pupil says teen number name when shown numerals – not in order) 11 12 13 14 15 16 17 18 19 20.	
39. Build a teen number with Numicon Shapes or Rods in response to seeing the numeral 11 12 13 14 15 16 17 18 19 20.	
40. Build a teen number with Numicon Shapes or Rods in response to hearing the number name 11 12 13 14 15 16 17 18 19 20.	
41. Name teen numbers built with Numicon Shapes or Rods 11 12 13 14 15 16 17 18 19 20.	
42. Write teen numbers in response to hearing the number.	
43. Write teen numbers in response to seeing them built with Shapes or Rods (not in order).	
44. Find the last number in a count to 20 on Numicon Number Line.	

Recognition of Shapes, counting and place value, continued

Pupil is able to	Comments
45. Say which is larger/smaller when looking at 2 numbers within 20.	
46. Find last number in a count to 20 on a 0-100 number line.	
47. Put a list of 4 random numerals within 20 in order.	
48. Find out how many to 20 without counting (by arranging into Numicon patterns) 11 12 13 14 15 16 17 18 19 20.	
49. Find 'teen' 'ty' numbers on number line without confusion (e.g. 15 and 50).	
50. Name and write any number to 100 built with Numicon Shapes or Number Rods (some pupils may need to work first to 30 and then 40 before they can do this with higher numbers).	
51. Build any number to 100 with Numicon Shapes or Number Rods in response to hearing and seeing the number name (some pupils may need to work first to 30 and then 40 before they can do this with higher numbers).	
52. Name any numeral to 100 (pupil says number name when shown numerals – not in order).	
53. Write any numeral to 100 (or pupil points to numeral) in response to hearing number name – not in order (some pupils may need to work first to 30 and then 40 before they can do this with higher numbers).	
54. Say which is larger/smaller when looking at two 2-digit numbers within 100.	
55. Recall half of 2 4 6 8 10. With Numicon Shapes or Number Rods show half of 12 14 16 18 20 and recall.	
56. Put a list of 7 random numerals beyond 20 in order (smallest to largest and largest to smallest).	
57. Mentally work out half of 20 40 60 80 100.	
58. Show half of 30 50 70 90 using Numicon Shapes or Number Rods.	

Working beyond 100 pupil uses structured apparatus to: 1) build numbers to 1000, 2) name numbers, 3) recognise, say and write numbers

Pupil is able to:	Comments
59. Build any number to 1000 with structured apparatus in response to hearing and seeing the number (some pupils may need work step by step 100-121 and then to 200 before moving to higher numbers)	
60. Name and write any number to 1000 built with structured apparatus (some pupils may need work step by step 100-121 and then to 200 before moving to higher numbers)	
61. Read any number to 1000	
62. Say which is larger/smaller when looking at two 3-digit numbers within 1000	
63. Put a list of 7 random numerals beyond 100 in order (smallest to largest and largest to smallest)	

Using Pattern

Pattern, order and sequence

Pupil is able to:	Comments
1. Show understanding of language of size and comparison: Bigger, biggest Smaller, smallest Larger, largest, Longer, longest Shorter, shortest Taller, tallest Heaviest, lightest.	
2. Use comparative language when comparing two Numicon Shapes or Number Rods.	
3. Use language of size/comparison.	
4. Understand language of position: on, in, top, bottom, side, next to, up, down, middle, outside, inside, above, below, before, after, first, last	
5. Use language of position.	
6. Order 3 objects according to size.	

Pattern, order and sequence

Pupil is able to:	Comments
7. Order more than 3 objects according to size.	
8. Order Numicon Shapes to…	
9. Order Number Rods to…	
10. Order Numicon Shapes 1-10.	
11. Order Number Rods 1-10.	
12. Copy an 'ab, ab'* pattern by matching.	
13. Copy and continue an 'ab, ab'* pattern	
14. Devise 'ab, ab'* patterns using a range of objects and apparatus.	
15. Copy an 'abc, abc'** pattern.	
16. Copy and continue an 'abc, abc'** pattern.	
17. Devise 'abc, abc' patterns using a range of objects and apparatus.	
18. Copy, continue and devise an extended range of repeating patterns, e.g. abb, abb; aabb, aabb.	
19. Copy, continue and devise patterns in P.E., Music and Art.	
20. Record simple repeating patterns (colouring, printing, drawing).	
21. Show awareness of pattern in the world around them.	

* 'ab ab' means alternating pattern e.g red blue red blue.
** 'abc abc' means repeating a sequence of three elements.

Pattern, order and sequence

Pupil is able to:	Comments
22. Show a '1 more' pattern with Numicon Shapes or Rods.	
23. Use Numicon Shapes or Rods to explain a '1 less' pattern.	
24. Copy and continue an abb, abb pattern arranged vertically.	
25. Devise an abb, abb pattern arranged vertically.	
26. Copy and continue an abbccc, abbccc pattern arranged vertically.	
27. Devise an abbccc, abbccc pattern arranged vertically.	
28. Record patterns by colouring.	
29. Assign numbers to repeating patterns (see Kit 1 Using Pattern Card 2A).	
30. Continue the sequence of assigned numbers in these patterns.	
31. Copy and continue a symmetrical pattern e.g. abbccc, cccbba pattern.	
32. Copy and continue a 'descending pattern' e.g. cccbba, cccbba pattern.	
33. Build a 'descending pattern' independently.	
34. Assign numbers to 'descending pattern'.	
35. Continue sequence of assigned numbers in 'descending patterns'.	
36. Devise symmetrical patterns.	

Pattern, order and sequence

Pupil is able to:	Comments
37. Record symmetrical patterns by colouring.	
38. Assign numbers to symmetrical patterns.	
39. Continue sequence of assigned numbers in symmetrical patterns.	
40. Build, record and assign numerals to an even numbers pattern (and predict next number).	
41. Build, record and assign numerals to an odd numbers pattern (and predict next number).	
42. Build, record and assign additions to a '1 more' pattern (1 + 1, 2 + 1, 3 + 1 etc.).	
43. Build, record and assign subtractions to a '1 less' pattern' (10 – 1, 9 – 1, 8 – 1 etc.).	
44. Respond to = by saying 'equals' or 'balances' and make the action for the sign.	
45. Use = in response to an equivalence shown with Numicon Shapes in a Pan Balance.	
46. Record the above using + = e.g. 5 + 4 = 9 and 9 = 4 + 5.	
47. Build and order addition facts of all numbers to 10 and explain what they have done.	
48. Record the above using + =.	
49. Show subtraction facts of all numbers to 10 in order and explain what they have done.	
50. Record the above using – =.	
51. Predict subsequent additions from the pattern 1 + 9, 2 + 8, 3 + 7 etc.	

Pattern, order and sequence

Pupil is able to:	Comments
52. Predict subsequent subtractions from the pattern 10 – 1, 10 – 2, 10 – 3 etc.	
53. Solve additions with empty box notation using Pan Balance.	
54. Record the above using + =.	
55. Devise equivalent additions and subtractions within their working range e.g. 3 + 3 = 9 – 6; 7 + 3 = 13 – 3; 30 + 30 = 90 – 60.	

Sequences using the Number Line: Working within 100 using Numicon Shapes and the Numicon Tens Number Line

Pupil is able to:	Comments
56. Build with Numicon Shapes and recite the sequence of 10's (starting at 0).	
57. From the sequence of Shapes, write down the sequence of 10's numerically (starting at 0).	
58. Build with Numicon Shapes and recite the sequence of 5's (starting at 0).	
59. From the sequence of Shapes, write down the sequence of 5's numerically (starting at 0).	
60. Build with Numicon Shapes and recite the sequence of 3's (starting at 0).	
61. From the sequence of Shapes, write down the sequence of 3's numerically (starting at 0).	
62. Build sequences with Numicon in response to written number sequences 10's, 5's, 3's, 2's.	

Working within 100 without Numicon apparatus

Pupil is able to:	Comments
63. Recognise and continue to record a forward sequence of odd numbers (starting at 1).	

Working within 100 without Numicon apparatus

Pupil is able to:	Comments
64. Recognise and continue to record a forward sequence of even numbers (starting at 0).	
65. Recognise and continue to record a backward sequence of odd numbers (starting at any odd number).	
66. Recognise and continue to record a backward sequence of even numbers (starting at any even number).	
67. Recognise and continue to record a forward sequence of 10's (starting at 0).	
68. Recognise and continue to record a backward sequence of 10 (starting at any multiple of 10)	
69. Recognise and continue to record a forward sequence of 10 (starting at any number).	
70. Recognise and continue to record a backward sequence of 10's (starting at any number).	
71. Recognise and continue to record a forward sequence of 5's (starting at zero).	
72. Recognise and continue to record a backward sequence of 5's (starting at any multiple of 5).	
73. Recognise and continue to record a forward sequence of 3's (starting at zero).	
74. Recognise and continue to record a backward sequence of 3's (starting at any multiple of 3).	

Working within 100 on forward missing number sequences that start at 0

Pupil is able to:	Comments
75. Find missing numbers in a forward sequence of odd numbers.	
76. Find missing numbers in a forward sequence of even numbers.	
77. Find missing numbers in a forward sequence of 10's.	

Working within 100 on forward missing number sequences that start at 0

Pupil is able to:	Comments
78. Find missing numbers in a forward sequence of 10's (starting at any number).	
79. Find missing numbers in a forward sequence of 5's.	
80. Find missing numbers in a forward sequence of 3's.	
81. Find missing numbers in a backward sequence of odd numbers (starting from any odd number).	
82. Find missing numbers in a backward sequence of even numbers (starting from any even number).	
83. Find missing numbers in a backward sequence of 10s (starting from any multiple of 10).	
84. Find missing numbers in a backward sequence of 10s (starting at any number).	
85. Find missing numbers in a backward sequence of 5s (starting from any multiple of 5).	
86. Find missing numbers in a backward sequence of 3s (starting from any multiple of 3).	

Working up to 1000 on forward and backward sequences of 50 and 25

Pupil is able to:	Comments
87. Repeat forward and backward sequences as above beyond 100	
88. Recognise, continue and record a forward sequence of 50s (starting at 0)	
89. Recognise, continue and record a backward sequence of 50s starting at any multiple of 50.	
90. Recognise, continue and record a forward sequence of 25s starting at 0.	
91. Recognise, continue and record a backward sequence of 25s starting at any multiple of 25.	

Calculating

Addition, subtraction, multiplication and division

Pupil is able to:	Comments
1. Respond to numbers and mathematical ideas in rhymes and stories.	
2. Begin to use language of arithmetic (and, more, take away, makes etc).	

Practical addition within 10 without counting

Pupil is able to:	Comments
3. When using Numicon, demonstrate awareness that numbers can be combined to make a larger one.	
4. Combine any two numbers totalling within 10, without counting, using Numicon Shapes or Number Rods and explain what they have done.	
5. Use Numicon Shapes or Number Rods to make an addition, in response to: How can you make 7?, Can you add 4 and 5?	
6. Respond to a story arithmetically e.g. when asked "two ducks on the pond and two more joined them" replies, "2 and/add 2 equals 4".	
7. Use Numicon Shapes or Number Rods to create story e.g. combine 2-Shape and 3-Shape and say e.g. "there were two pupils playing and three more came to join in so there were five altogether".	
8. Begin to mentally recall all addition facts within 10 without apparatus.	
9. Respond to + sign by saying 'and' add, 'plus' and make the action for the sign.	
10. Read aloud a written addition and demonstrate with Numicon Shapes or Number Rods.	
11. Use Numicon Shapes or Number Rods to build an addition and write the sum.	
12. Respond to story with an addition e.g. respond to two ducks on the pond and two more swam up to them, by writing 2 + 2 = 4.	

Practical addition within 10 without counting, continued

Pupil is able to:	Comments
13. Create a story from a written addition e.g. responds to 4 + 2 = 6 by saying, "there were four snails crawling along the top of the wall and two crawling along the bottom, so there were six snails altogether".	
14. Show understanding that addition is commutative.	
15. Mentally recall addition facts within 10 without apparatus.	

Practical subtraction within 10 without counting

Pupil is able to:	Comments
16. When using Numicon show awareness that subtraction from a number results in a smaller number.	
17. Show subtraction (as take away) with Numicon or Number Rods and explain using vocabulary involved in taking away.	
18. Recognise the difference between two numbers within 10 using Numicon Shapes or Number Rods.	
19. Show subtraction (as comparison and difference) with Numicon Shapes or Number Rods and explain using vocabulary involved in comparing.	
20. Use Numicon Shapes or Number Rods to show a subtraction, in response to: How can you show 7 take away 3?, Can you take away 4 from 10?, Can you show the difference between 10 and 8?	
21. Respond to a subtraction story e.g. when asked "there were three cars in a car park and one was driven away. How many were left?" replies '3 take away 1 equals 2".	
22. Create a take away story and illustrate it with Numicon Shapes or Number Rods e.g. "I had ten sweets and I ate four, so I only have six left.", by taking the 10-Shape and hiding 4.	
23. Begin to mentally recall subtraction facts.	
24. Respond to – sign by saying 'take away', 'subtract', 'the difference between' and make the action for the sign.	
25. Read aloud a written subtraction and demonstrate with Numicon Shapes or Number Rods.	
26. Use Numicon Shapes or Number Rods to show a subtraction and write it.	

Practical subtraction within 10 without counting, continued

Pupil is able to:	Comments
27. Respond to story with a subtraction e.g. respond to six ducks on the pond and two swam away by writing 6 – 2 = 4.	
28. Create a story from a written subtraction e.g. responds to 3 – 1, by saying, "three apples on a plate one was eaten, how many were left".	
29. Recall mentally subtraction facts within 10 without Numicon.	

Calculating with numbers higher than 10

(Note: at each of the higher number stages should be able to respond to stories/problems arithmetically and compose arithmetic problems)

Pupil is able to:	Comments
30. Add and subtract whole tens e.g. 50 ± 30.	
31. Add and subtract U to/from TU without crossing 10s e.g. 56 ± 3.	
32. Add and subtract whole tens to/from TU e.g. 64 ± 10, (also ± 30).	
33. Add and subtract completing to multiples of 10 e.g. 58 + 2, 83 – 3.	
34. Add or subtract units to/from units up to 20 e.g. 9 + 6, 16 – 7.	
35. Recall double facts of 6 7 8 9 10.	
36. Add or subtract U to/from TU crossing 10s e.g. 58 + 7, 63 – 5.	
37. Add or subtract TU and TU without crossing 10s e.g. 56 ± 33.	
38. Recall mentally doubles of multiples of 5.	
39. Add and subtract TU and TU crossing tens e.g. 56 ± 37.	

Multiplication

Pupil is able to:	Comments
40. Use Numicon to show multiplication and explain using language of multiplication.	
41. Respond to x sign by making the action for the sign in multiplications and using language.	
42. Read a written multiplication and build it with Numicon Shapes or Number Rods.	
43. Respond to a multiplication story e.g. when asked "there were three bicycles ridden along the road, how many wheels?" replies, '3 times 2 equals 6' and writes 3 x 2 = 6.	
44. Create a multiplication story.	
45. Show understanding that multiplication is commutative.	
46. Mentally recall multiplication facts, 2s, 5s and 10s.	

Division

Pupil is able to:	Comments
47. Use Numicon to show division and explain using language of division.	
48. Respond to ÷ sign by making the action for the sign in division questions and using language.	
49. Read a written division and show with Numicon Shapes or Number Rods.	
50. Respond to a division story e.g. when asked "ten pencils shared between two people, how many each?" replies 'Ten divided into two equals five' and writes 10 ÷ 2 = 5.	
51. Create a division story.	
52. Read division and use the inverse of multiplication to solve it.	
53. Solve a division with a remainder using Numicon Shapes or Number Rods e.g. 10 ÷ 3 = 3 remainder 1.	
54. Mentally recall division facts of 2s, 5s and 10s. Begin to mentally recall division facts of 3s and 4s.	

Assessment Tool 3: Pupil Profile

This Assessment Tool should be used to build a picture of a pupil's strengths and difficulties in order to highlight the mathematical teaching strategies and Numicon Activities that should be used to address these needs. The form is in two sections, to show a pupil's level of mathematical understanding *and* ability to access mathematical teaching. The initial profile will help provide a framework for planning intervention and learning support and will inform reviews of a pupil's progress.

Profiling is likely to be most useful if it is undertaken by a multidisciplinary team (e.g. teacher, speech and language therapist, educational psychologist and maths consultant) and will help to facilitate effective, individualised learning. We strongly advise that teachers avoid labelling a pupil's needs in order to match them with strategies assigned to that label.

Pupil's Name: DOB: NC Year:

Names and positions of those compiling this profile: Date:

Level of mathematical understanding

Area of mathematics	Strengths	Needs	Numicon activity/mathematical teaching strategies
Pattern awareness			
Knowledge of number order/counting			
Knowledge of numbers and place value notation/place value			
Addition			
Subtraction			
Mathematical thinking (reasoning, generalising, working systematically, application)			

Ability to access mathematical teaching

Area of mathematics	Strengths	Needs	Numicon activity/mathematical teaching strategies
Language of mathematics			
Attention control and listening			
Memory			
Motor organisation			
Language of mathematics (sound structure)			
Confidence/anxiety			
Participation/passivity			

Index

The following pages feature the Photocopy Masters referred to throughout the Closing the Gap with Numicon Activities

One to One Correspondence

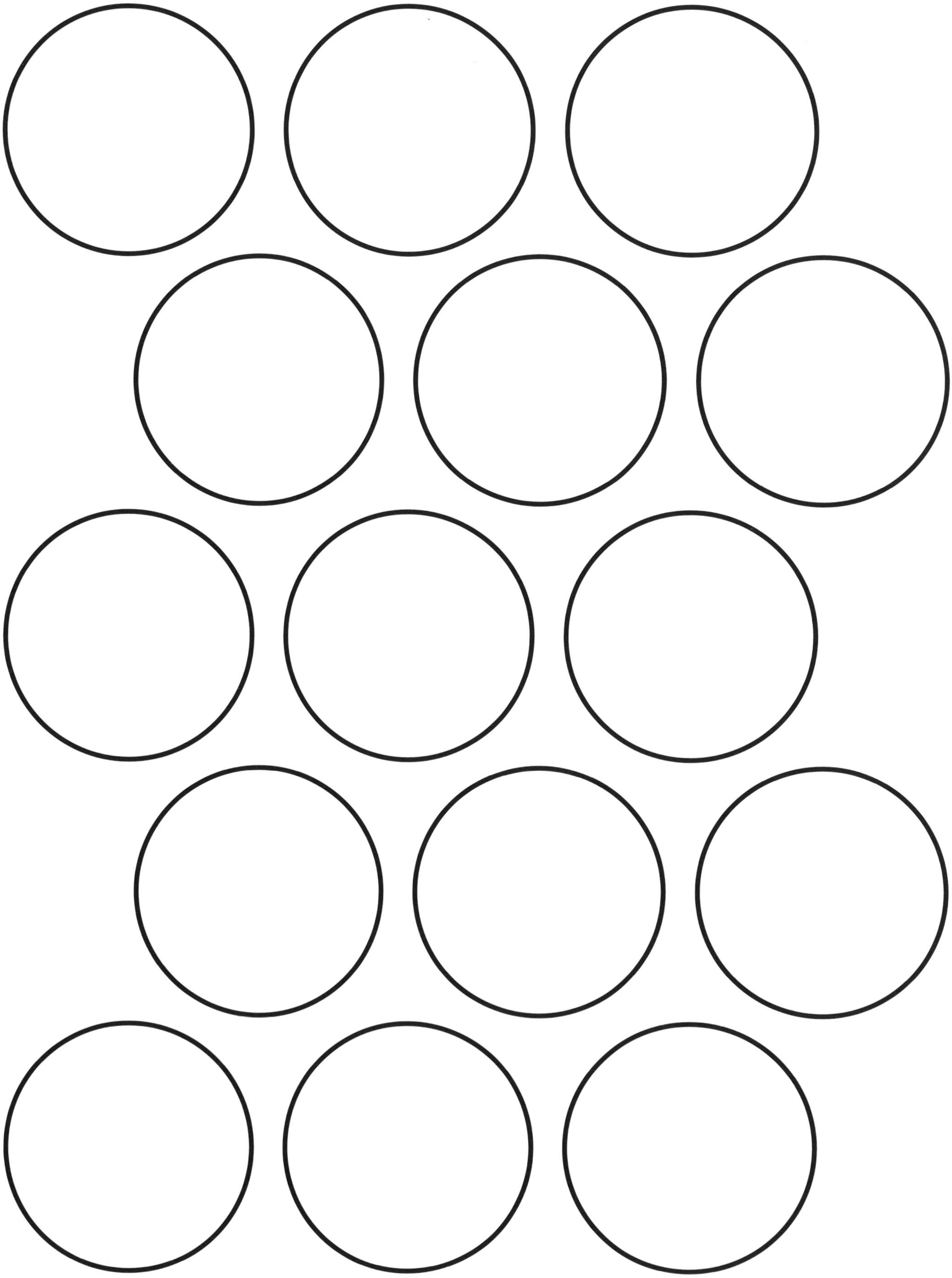

Outline Numicon Shapes

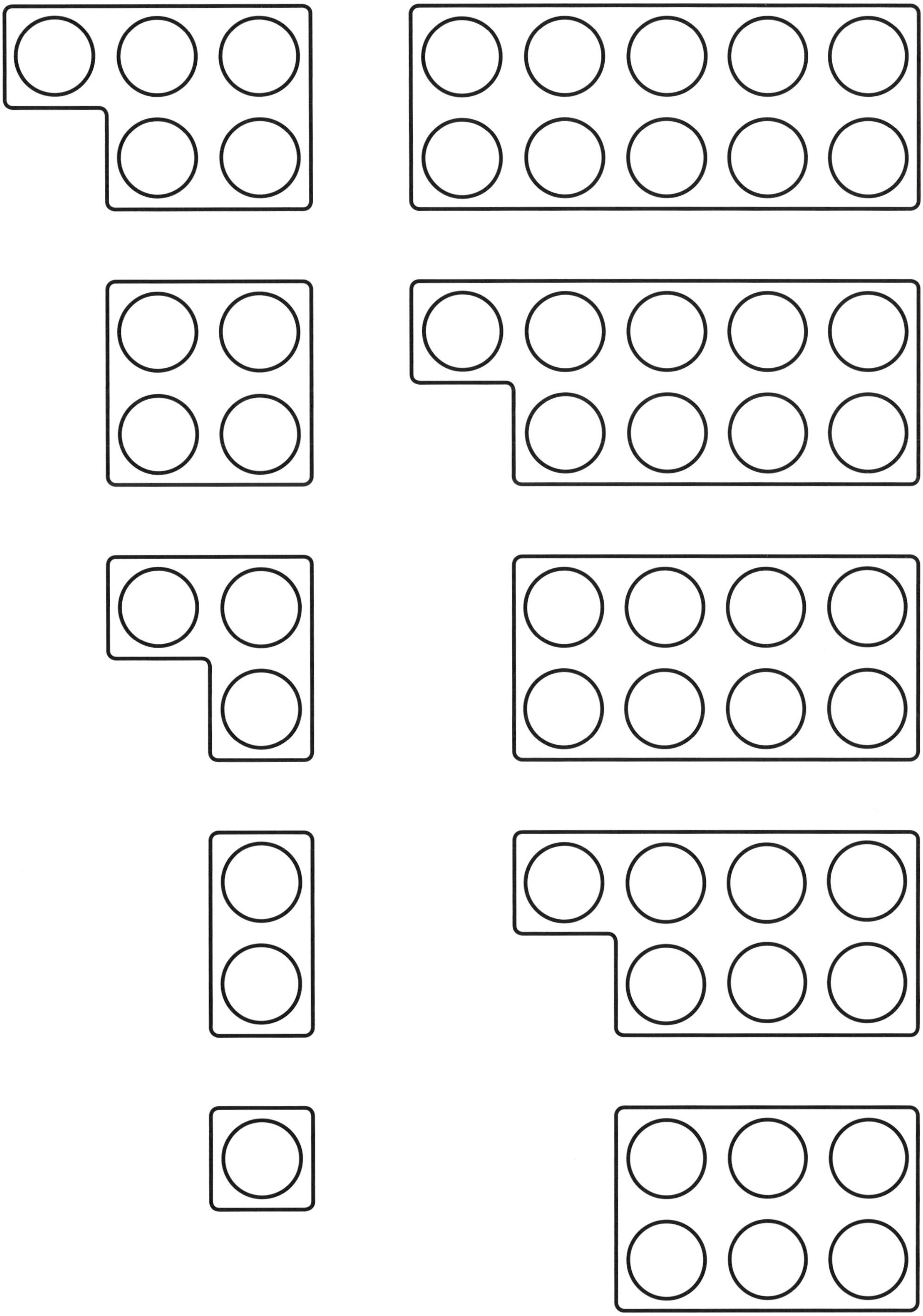

0-10 Number Line

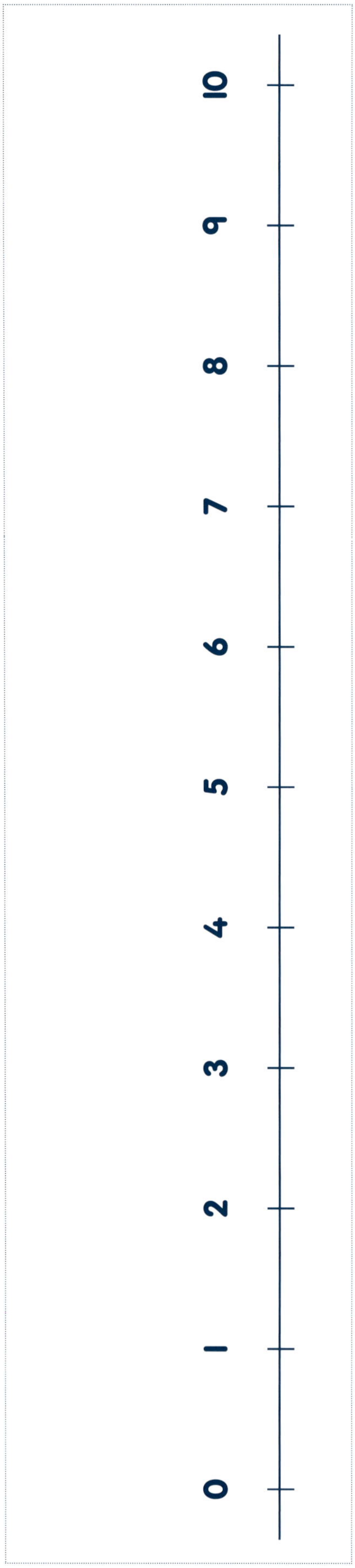

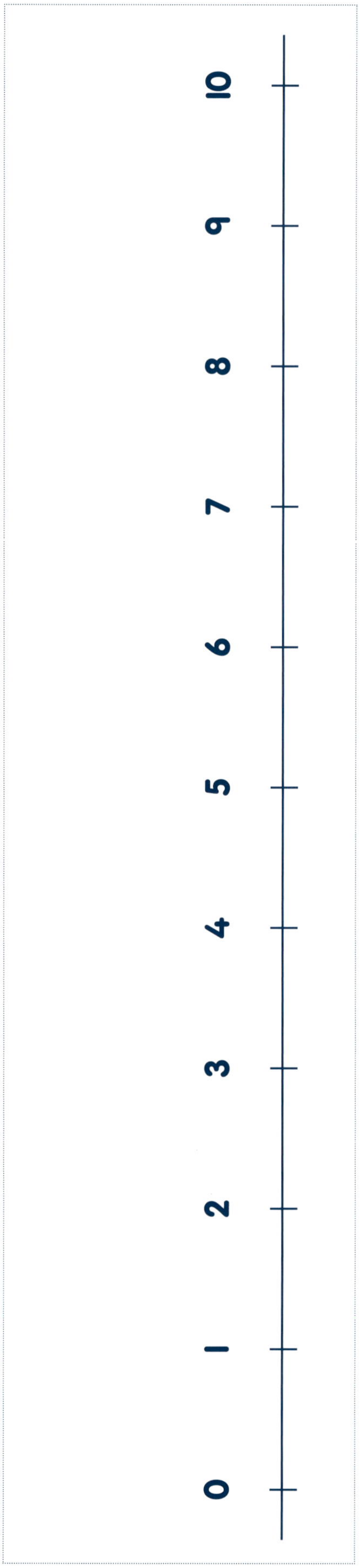

Number Track

AFFIX NEXT SECTION (11-20)

10
9
8
7
6
5
4
3
2
1
0

AFFIX NEXT SECTION (21-30)

20
19
18
17
16
15
14
13
12
11

30
29
28
27
26
25
24
23
22
21

Ordering Frame

COPY THIS PAGE TWICE AND JOIN ORDERING FRAMES ALONG THIS EDGE

Spinner Overlays 1

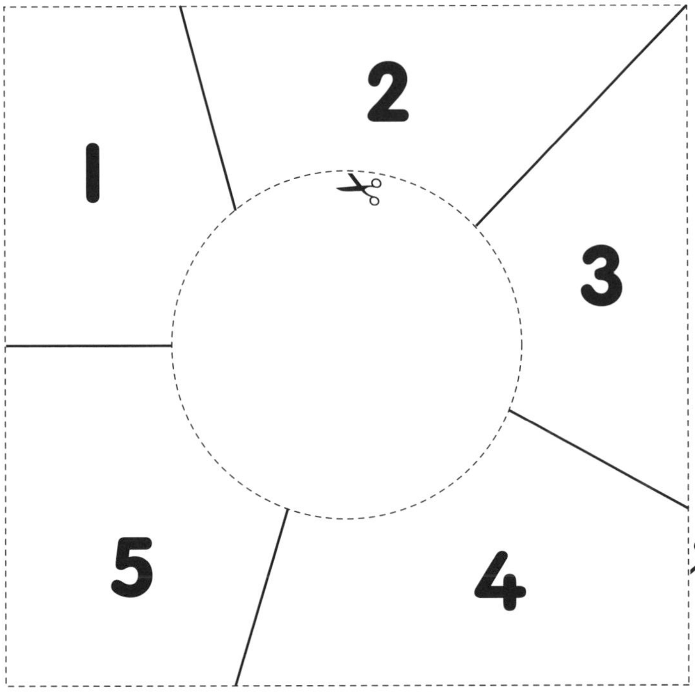

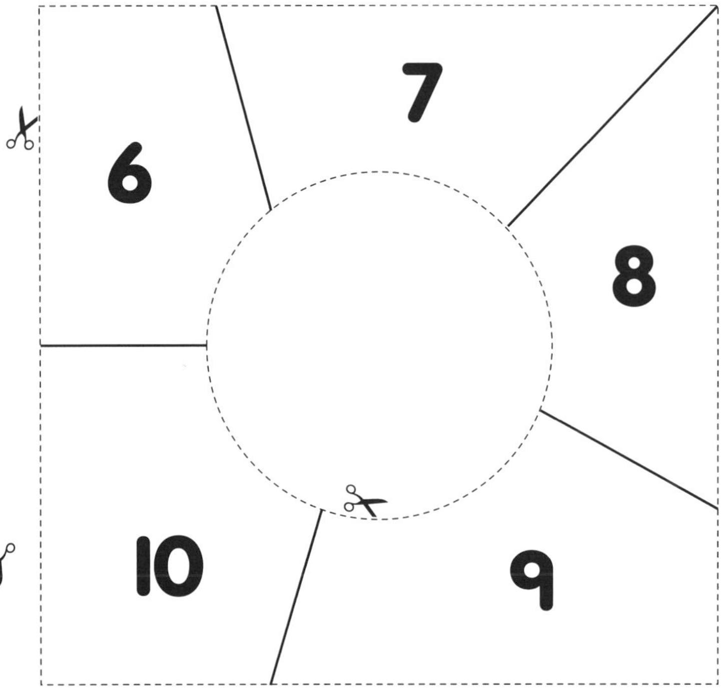

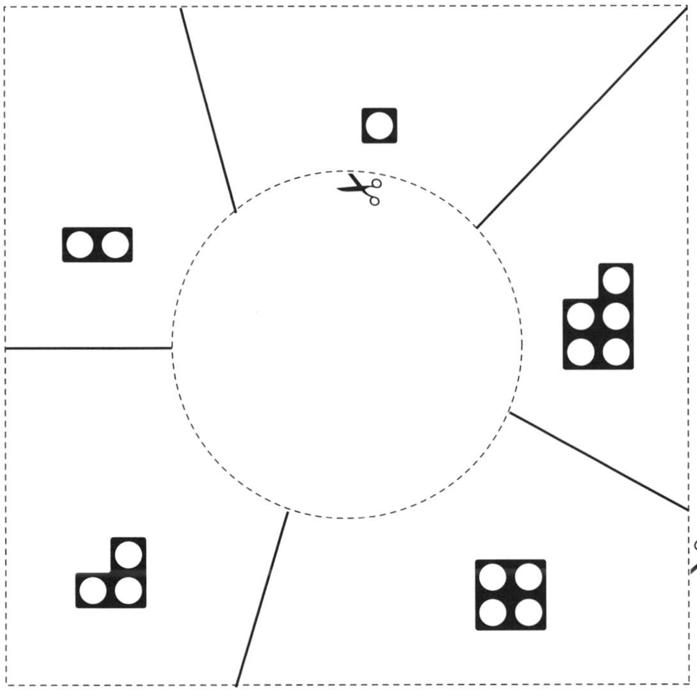

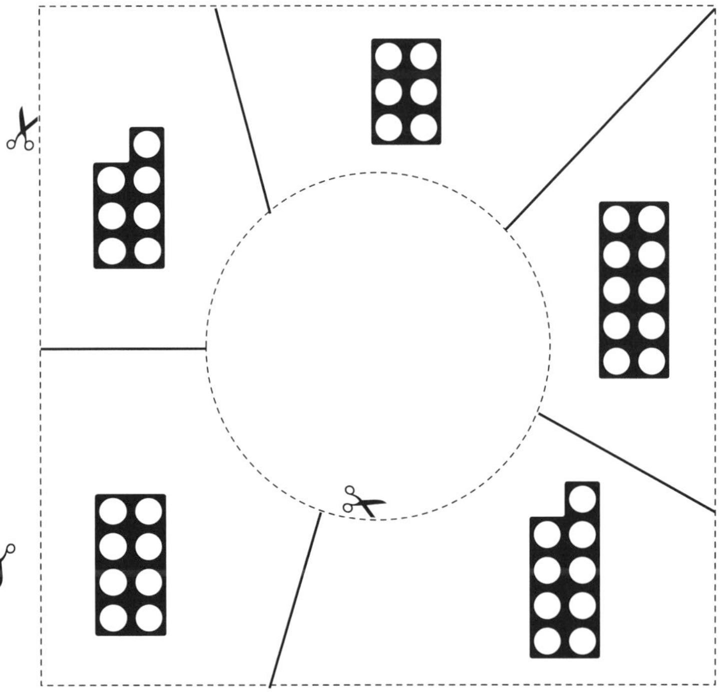

Spinner Overlays 2

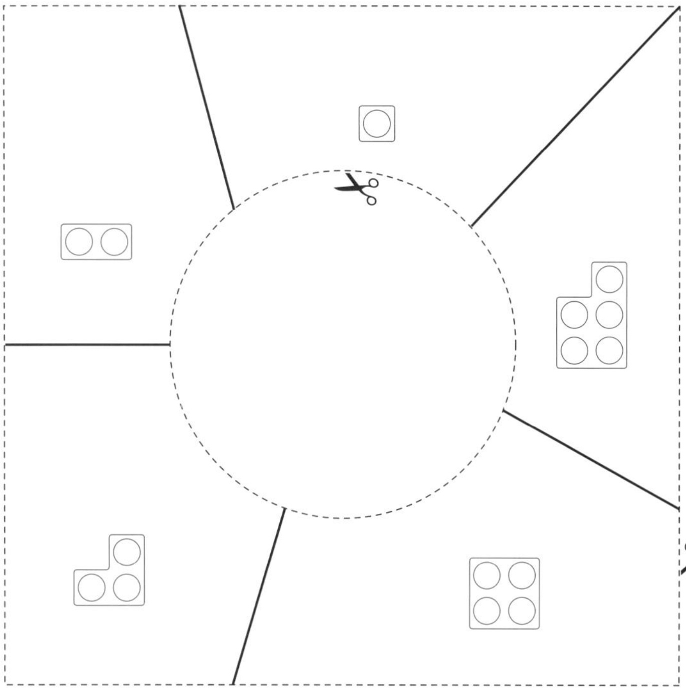

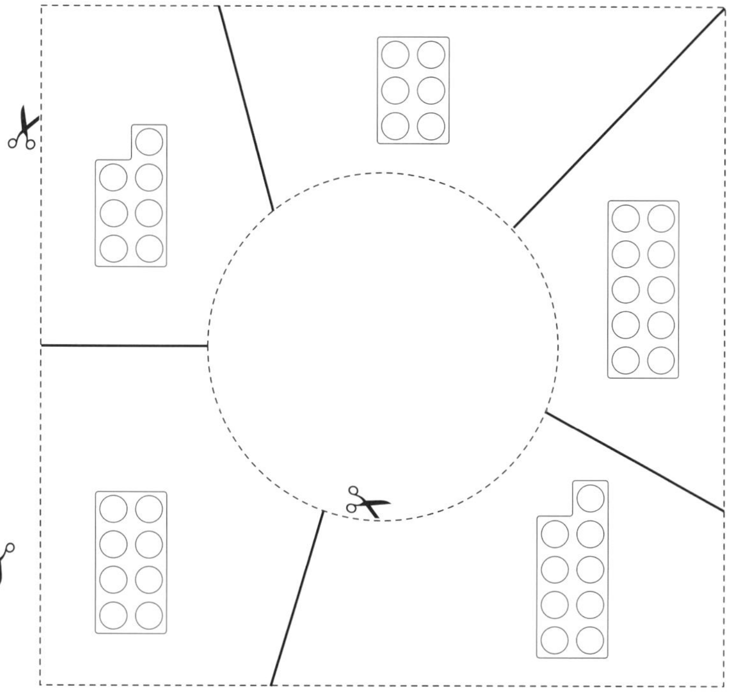

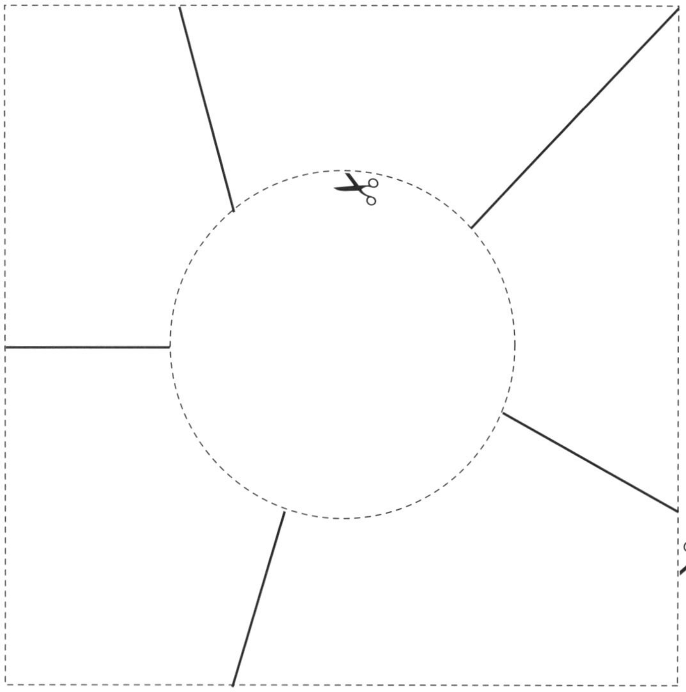

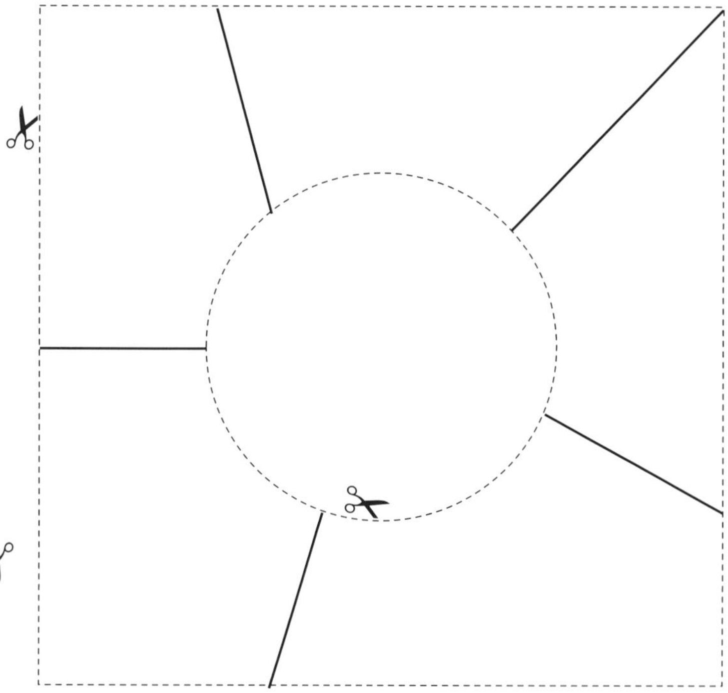

'Baseboard' – For drawing shapes and patterns

2cm Squared Paper – choose scale according to pupil's needs. Enlarge if necessary.

1.5cm Squared Paper – choose scale according to pupil's needs. Enlarge if necessary.

Numeral Cards 0-10

0 numicon	1 numicon	2 numicon
3 numicon	4 numicon	5 numicon
6 numicon	7 numicon	8 numicon
9 numicon	10 numicon	

Plasticine Master 1-5

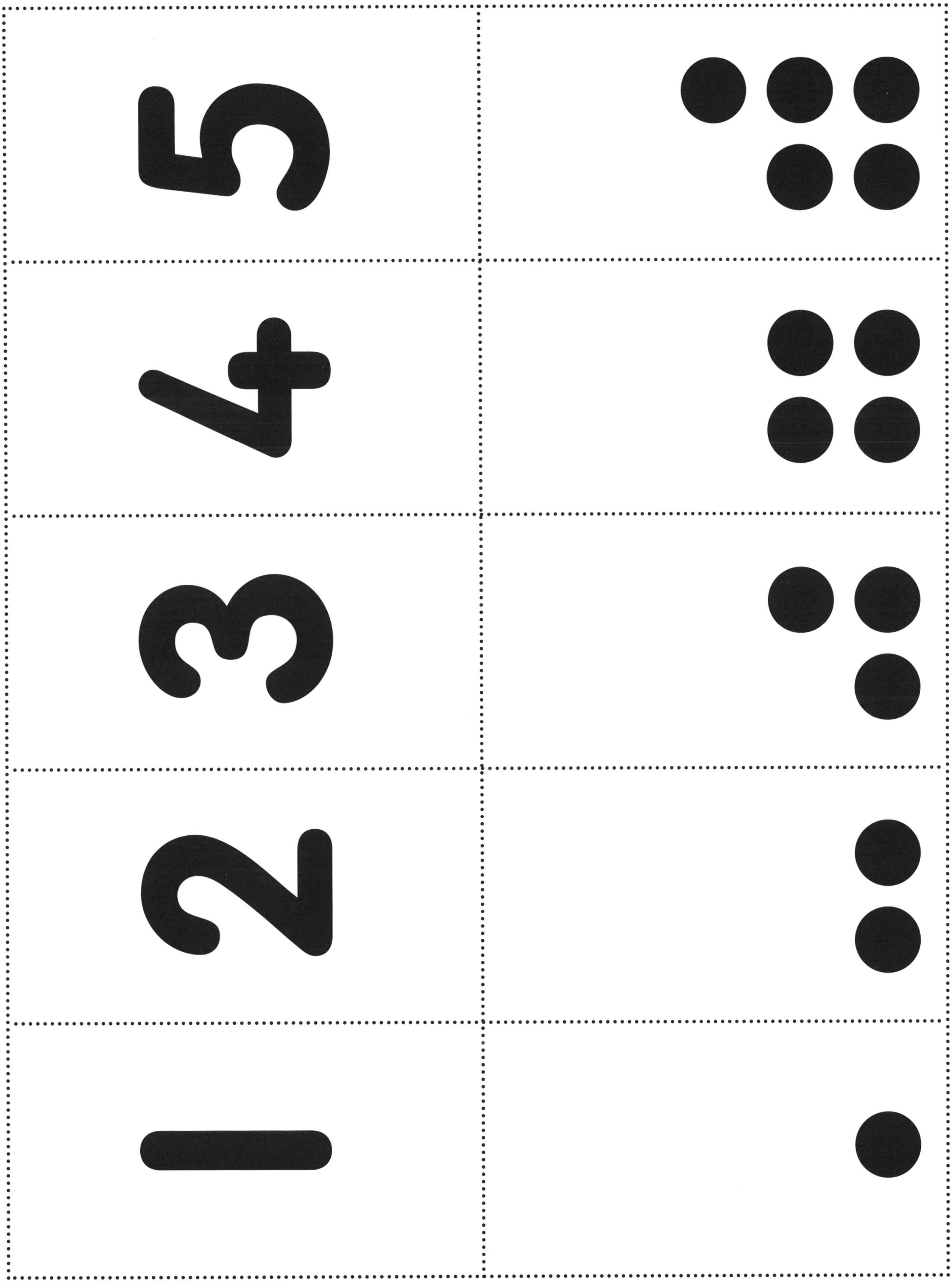

Plasticine Master 6-10

10

9

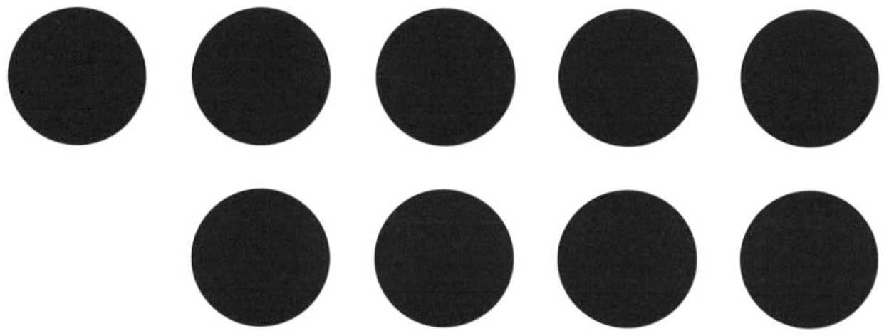

8

7

6

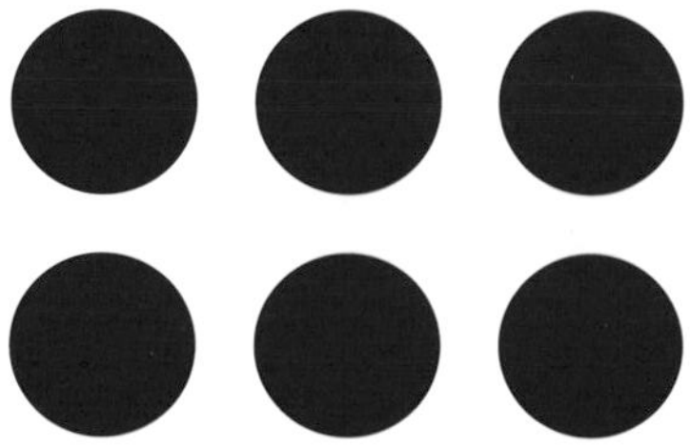

Part/Whole Frames

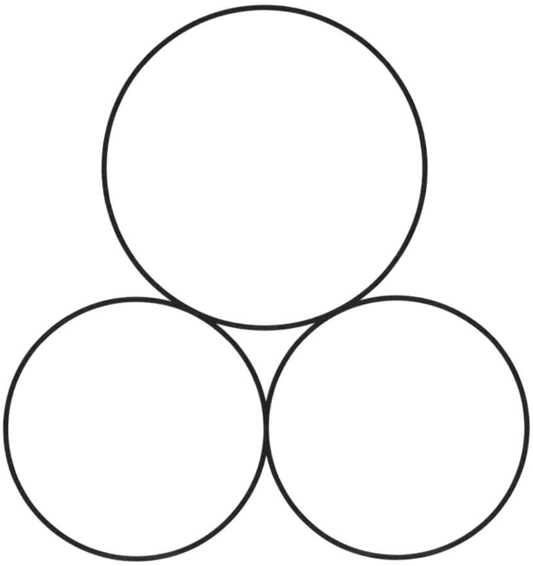

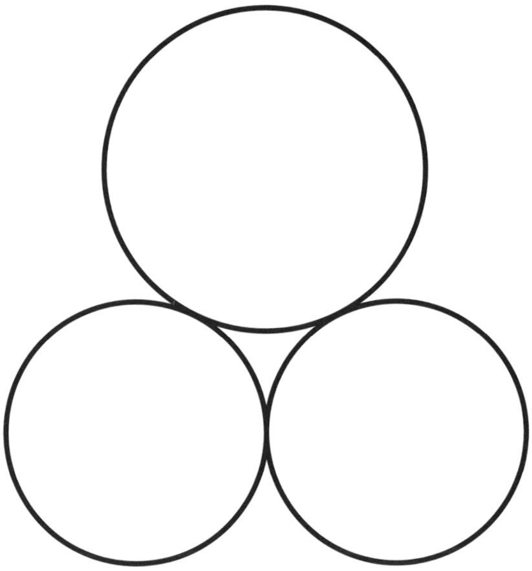

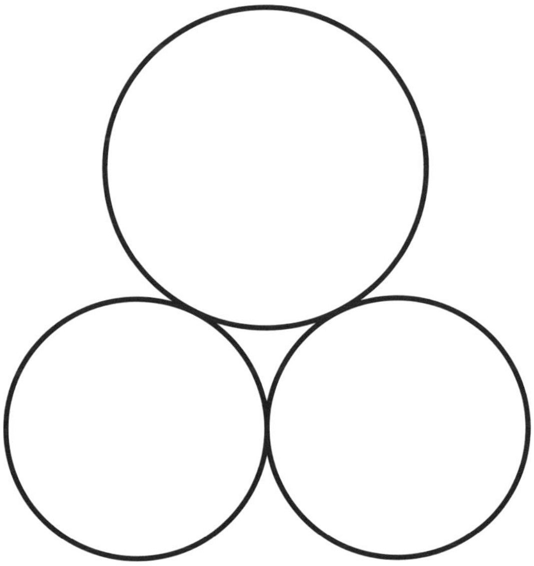

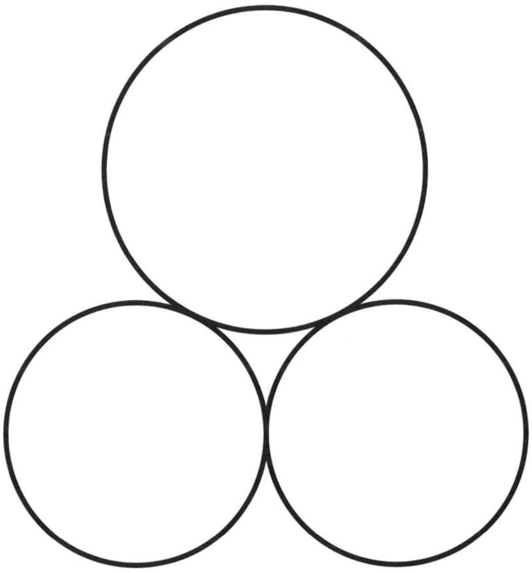

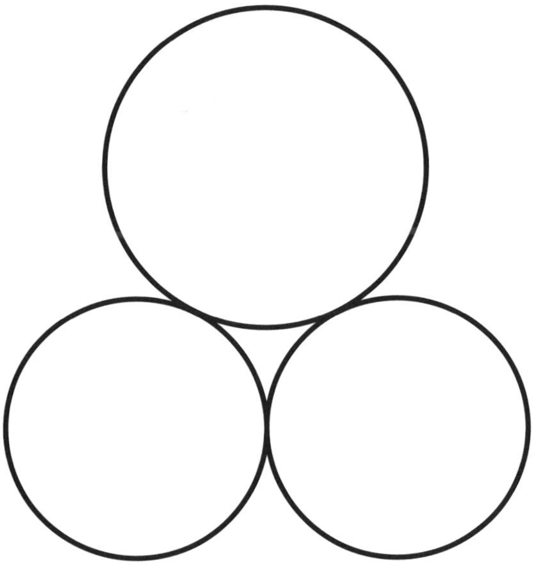

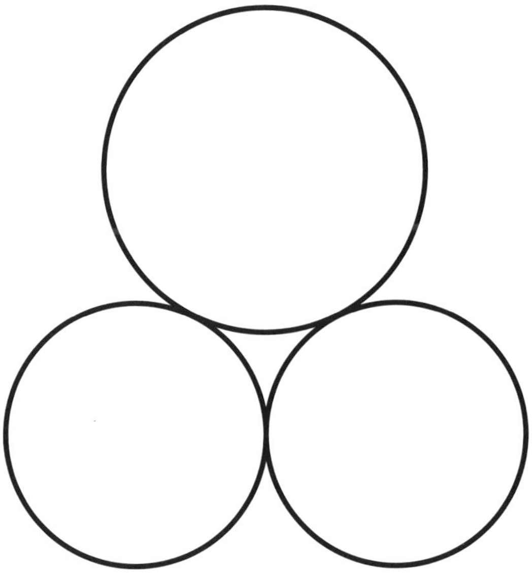

Making

	and	
	and	
	and	
	and	
	and	
	and	
	and	
	and	
	and	
	and	

Subtraction Covers 1-5

Subtraction Covers 6-10